D1524179

Bad bOys On VideO

Interviews With gay adult stars

by Mickey Skee

Cover photo of Jeff Palmer, courtesy Falcon Studios

Copyright © 1998 by Mickey Skee

COMPANION PRESS
PO Box 2575, Laguna Hills, California 92654

Printed in the United States of America
First Printing 1998

ISBN: 1-889138-12-6

Contents

To the master, the historian, my mentor, Jerry Douglas—
you taught me how to be fair, stand firm and stay above the fray.

Acknowledgments

ONCE AGAIN, IT'S IMPOSSIBLE TO thank everyone who helped me with this, but "important big thanks and hugs" go to Freddie Bercovitz and Patryk Strait at Video 10, Michael Christopher at BIG Video, Coy Dekker, Karen Dior, Allan Gassman and Mr. Eddie, Bob East and Faron at Men of Odyssey, Kevin Clarke and the Jaguar Studios boys, Marci Hirsch at Vivid, Colin Harris, Chuck Holmes, Shantay and John Rutherford at Falcon, Debbie Rubio at HIS/VCA, Scott Masters and John Travis at Studio 2000, Gino Colbert at New Age Pictures, Stephen Mounce and Tom Walker at Catalina, and to those fabu stars Peter Dixon, Adam Hart and Cole Tucker for getting all their photos to me in a moment's notice.

Thanks to my assistant, Melissa, who took time from her holiday skiing trip to help me transcribe these tapes. See, now you've made it into one of these porn books, Missy! And thank you to my best friend Sharon Kane and her pig Candy for keeping me company and bringing me coffee during the wee hours of the night while I was working on this.

Thanks to Jim Buck for coming out to my house from New Orleans, and to Derek Cameron for meeting me at a coffeehouse on a cool morning the day before this book was due. Thanks to my pals Big Daddy Ferguson and Hank Ferguson from *Gay Chicago*; J.C. Adams, Jordon Sable, Sabin, Tim Evanson, Joe Molsby (muscular@ aol.com), and Jerry Douglas from *Manshots*; Gary Philipp from *Skinflicks*; Jack Francis and John Erich from *Unzipped;* and ANT from *Twink* for helping me with your necessary support and knowledge.

To all the great new directors I've met this year: Wash West, Lucas Kazan and Jett Blakk; and to some of the oldtimers I've met for the first time, such as Bill Higgins, Barry Knight and Russell Moore—thanks. Much thanks also to Montana, Mocha, Rolf and all the photographers who helped me and who help keep this business rolling.

To the stars who trekked to my house: Scott Baldwin, Adam Hart, Jason Miller, Rex Chandler, Steve O'Donnell, Jeff Palmer, Tanner Reeves, Marco Rossi—all of you—thanks a great deal for making it up to the Hollywood Hills to see me for interviews (and walking all 39 steps).

Derrick Stanton, Steve Rambo, Scott Randsome, Sonny Markham,

Adam Rom, Eduardo—thanks for taking time out of your busy schedules to spend many hours with me (Scott on your birthday, yet!).

A special heartfelt thanks to Will Clark and Dino Phillips, two of my closest buds in the biz. You deserve to be in this book whether we're friends or not, and thanks for doing last-minute work for me to help get this book together.

You were all so real and honest with me. I hope the fans will love and respect you as much as I do.

Introduction

How does one pick the best and hottest *Men of the Year* from the most handsome, erotic guys on the planet? I don't know. It's a daunting task, and I'm trying my best.

And, why should you listen to me? Good question. **Shooting Porn**, the Golden Satellite award-nominated documentary about the gay adult industry named me "the leading expert in the gay porn world." That scares me, frankly. Because I'm the Gay Editor of the *"Variety"* of porn, *Adult Video News*, and senior porn reviewer for *Twink*, *URGE* magazine, the *XXX Gay Film Guide*, the *Gay Video Guide*, The *AVN Annual Gay Supplement* and *Anything that Moves* and an occasional contributor to *Manshots*, *Skinflicks*, *Frontiers* and *Thrust*, folks out there think I know something about porn. Who knows? *Attitude* magazine just included me among the Top 10 Most Influential in Porn. Who the fuck cares?

Plenty of guys belong in this book as the *Men of the Year*, but I'm bringing you the most fascinating cross-section I can compile. That's why there'll be plenty of sequels to this book, until I can cover everyone who

I know deserves to be profiled.

When my publisher told me he wanted an interview book about the hottest hunks in porn, I said I easily had 100 screen studs to put in it. When I had to narrow it down to 20, it was like picking out a favorite lube.

So, I've included a big range of men. Some are dark, some are light, some with short cropped hair, some with long flowing locks. Some live on the West Coast, some in the East, North, South and Midwest. Some have accents, some speak other languages, some speak deep, some squeak. They range from 5-foot, 7-inches all the way up to 6-foot, 5-inches in height. Some work out five days a week, others don't work out at all. Some watch what they eat, some can eat anything—and do.

I know the details you want to hear. Yes, some are cut and some are uncut. Some have dicks as fat as their fists, some have long skinny cocks. And they range from seven inches of juicy cock to a full, genuine 10 inches. Some cum in handfuls, others in spurts. Some grunt, some howl, some whine.

Whatever your taste, your type, your kink, there's a guy in these pages to fill your fantasies. And they tell their own fantasies, too.

There're a few older than 40 and a few barely 21. There're a few who've retired from posing naked, but they're always there for us on our video screens. And, there're a few newcomers you've never heard of, but I'm banking on it that you will.

There're a few stars you've heard way too much about because they're on the brink of porn over-exposure, but within these pages I uncover stories that have never been told. Many of the interviews are first-time looks at the guys behind the cocks: where they came from, how they started and where they hope to go.

Some of the guys in the following pages are buffed and muscle-bound. Others are lean and skinny. Some are kinky, some are shy. Some were nasty, some would cry. Some are funny, some were serious. Some were witty, some delirious. Some are totally wild, some are relatively mild. Some are tops, some are bottoms, many are versatile. Some are almost totally shaved, some are so hairy they look like bears. Some have a little gray around their temples, some barely have pubic hair.

In the interviews you'll be able to tell that there are a few of the guys with whom I'm relatively familiar or know very well, while others I have met for the first time. Some of them have won so many awards they have to build a mantle to hold them, some of them haven't won a single trophy, yet.

What are some of these guys doing in this book? Rex Chandler and Scott Baldwin have retired, yes, and they're missed, but they are not forgotten and even had recent video releases and award wins, proving that the fans never forget.

Derrick Stanton is an old-timer who made a brief comeback, and audiences are thrilled he did. He's been in the business as long as newcomer Jason Miller has been alive! And now Derrick's retiring again.

Newcomer Jeff Palmer announces his retirement in these pages, and old-age newcomer Cole Tucker talks about how he is the oldest guy who ever joined the business, and how he juggles a successful career on the side.

Adam Rom and Tanner Reeves took some time off and are now back doing porn. Adam took time off for a boyfriend, Tanner took time off because he was almost killed.

Steady, dependable and always-working performers such as Dino Phillips, Eduardo, and Will Clark have been around for years and expect to continue to be. And new superstars such as Steve O'Donnell, Jim Buck and Sonny Markham just joined the A-list team and fans can't get enough of them.

Adam Hart, Rex Chandler, Derek Cameron, Jim Buck and Steve Rambo want to direct videos, and some have with great success. All of them have had a great time screwing for us on videotape, and all of them were very forthright and honest in their most revealing interviews to date.

What did we talk about? You name it. Religion, dating, family, haircuts, piercings, doing it with brothers, cousins and nephews, drugs, jobs, aliens, traveling, art, redecorating their houses, psychology, smoking, spirituality, school, hobbies, death and near-death experiences, philosophy, movies, pets, leather, cars, college and the future, dancing, clothes, dolls, teachers, children, coming out to the world as gay, walking, talk shows, horses, real estate, bicycles, birthdays and growing older, sports, cooking, books, coffee, writing and hard-ons at inappropriate times.

There's the story one star has about coming out to his family as a pornstar over dinner, and the story about being fucked for the first time while cameras are running. There're a few who admit for the first time they've enjoyed pussy, and a few who insist that they're straight. Some say they want children, some say they never want to settle down. Some say they want to fuck their fans, some admit to what they're looking for in a guy. Some came from overseas and some lived in Los Angeles all their lives. Some came from evangelist families or Catholic schools, some came from broken homes or closeknit large families.

Oh, and we talked about sex, too. We talked about their first times masturbating, their first cumshots, their first fucks.

We talked about their foreskins, their hairy balls, their tight butts, their sexy eyebrows, their rockhard abs, their seductive eyes, their thick thighs, their beefy biceps, their long eyelashes, their pubic hair trims.

We discussed dildos, condoms and boyfriends. We dished about directors, co-stars and cockrings. There're secrets about getting it up, keeping it up, keeping it in, keeping it clean and working it up.

The stars also share inside information about getting in the biz.

They told me things they would not tell their boyfriends, girlfriends or wives—and stories they'd never tell their directors.

It's all here. Have fun, and remember, it's only Volume One.

If you have suggestions for the next volume you can write me at: PO Box 93309, Los Angeles, CA 90093.

Mickey Skee
Hollywood, California

Scott Baldwin

"I was a virgin. The first time I sucked was on film. The first time I got fucked was on film."

t was a sad day in porn when Scott Baldwin decided to give up sex on video and go off into the real world. The reason I wanted to include him in the first **Bad Boys On Video** is because although he retired, his video legacy lives on and fans still talk about his boyish charm and his sparkling smile.

Scott is also one of the first guys who made a super splash in such a short time in recent gay porn history. He had a one-two punch as Supporting Actor at both the Gay Erotic Video Awards in 1994 for **Flashpoint** and the 1995 *Adult Video News* Awards in Las Vegas. He won Best Erotic Scene for a hot steamy desert fuck with Brad Hunt in 100-degree heat in the back of a convertible for **Flashpoint** in 1995's Gay Erotic Video Awards, and in 1996 he picked up another Supporting Actor honor for **Our Trespasses**, in which he plays an innocent guy seeking absolution who gets seduced by a priest who once had a relationship with his father (also played by Baldwin).

The fans picked him as The Stud You'd Most Like to Fuck and Best Bottom at the Probe Men in Video Awards, the Probies, and he came close to winning Most Cuddly Stud and Best Comeback in 1996.

He was a nominee in 1994 for his role as a young buck seeking fame in the Big Apple in **Manhattan Skyline** and for the romantic fucking he did with Devyn Foster in **Prisoner of Love**.

"I guess I found something that I'm good at," said the endlessly precocious Scott (Scotty to his friends) when accepting his first Gay Erotic Video Award for Best Supporting performer in Falcon's **Flashpoint**. In that **Thelma & Louise** road video (of Theo and Louis), he abandons his gas station job and is picked up by a dark and handsome stranger, Hal Rockland, and later gang-raped in a bar.

In person, he's as cute, cuddly, intelligent and oh-so-sweet as he is on

Scott Baldwin

In **Flashpoint** and 100-degree heat.

Photo courtesy: Falcon Studios

screen. Visiting me at my house in the Hollywood Hills, this virgin from Virginia gave his last interview before stepping off into the real world of bookkeeping and marriage.

He revealed that he took the name "Baldwin" because he and his three brothers are also a handsome trio. His older brother is a police officer and his younger brother is simply gorgeous, but neither of them have had male-male sex, as far as he knows.

Scotty is an exhibitionist. Before fucking on film, he says, "the only thing I'd ever done before is streak in public with my fraternity. I used to run in public naked all the time." And no doubt, heads would turn.

His fantasy which he's yet to fulfill is: "I'd like to have a woman fuck me with a big strap-on. A lot of guys couldn't get into that, but I would."

He enjoys telling how he was discovered by literally being pulled off the street in his college town and asked to do videos. He's an aggressive bottom who loves to squeal, he's a masterful cocksucker with a winning smile and a good-old-boy persona packing a lot of beef.

He's worked with some of the biggest name directors in the business, Steven Scarborough, Sam Abdul, Jim Steel, Thor Stephens, Chi Chi La Rue, Josh Eliot, Ric Bradshaw and John Rutherford, at most of the major companies.

"I was there when he first put a dick in his mouth, the first time was on video," says director Rutherford, of Falcon Studios. The scene was with handsome blond hunk Tim Barnett, and it was awkward at first because Barnett packs such a monstrous cock, but Scott took it like a pro. "He wasn't sure what to do with his hands, but he got into it," Rutherford smiles. "He's a cuddly teddy bear—very, very sweet."

In one of his last public appearances in mid 1997, his buddy Chi Chi LaRue convinced him to dance off Time Square at the Eros Theater one last time with Jordan Young and the fans loved him.

He made one of the most recent big splashes into the all-male industry, and before we can even get used to him, he's left it, but not without leaving some fond memories.

"A lot of people think I'm an idiot. Maybe it's my Southern accent. I'm not stupid, I have my college degrees, and I like doing this," Scott says. "I figure I might as well do it while I'm young, but I'll never be ashamed of it, I'll always acknowledge that Scott Baldwin was a part of me. I have my whole life to sit behind a desk."

MICKEY: You seemed very shocked and surprised when you won your awards at the various shows these past two years. Did you have any idea you'd do so well?

SCOTT: Yeah, it was fun. I knew I'd win something because so many people were telling me I would. I was nominated for so many different awards, it's kinda overwhelming.

MICKEY: There were others who were nominated who didn't win anything. And you were one of the few with multiple nominations. You were in one of the biggest award-winning videos in recent history, and it's destined to be a classic. **Flashpoint** seemed like a lot of fun.

SCOTT: At that point I had made about a half dozen movies. **Flashpoint** was different because we got to hang out in San Francisco and then we all drove all the way down to the desert in these trailers like a caravan. It was like a big moving movie crew. The heat drove me crazy and we got to arguing. They told me to say we—Hal Rockland and I— were lovey-dovey all the time, but that's not true.

MICKEY: I heard that Falcon had a hard time keeping you and Hal Rockland apart at first, that you really were into each other.

SCOTT: He's a really nice person. They do try to keep people apart at first. I got over that pretty quickly, though. (*He smiles*)

MICKEY: And I also I heard you were literally walking down the street when you were discovered.

SCOTT: It was wild. I was walking through a mall. This was back in Virginia, where I'm from. I was with my best friend from college. Dave Crowell, an agent who is well known in the adult industry, ran out of the mall to find me at my car in the parking lot and asked if I wanted to do some sports modeling. At that time I had never been to a gay club and never had done anything, you know, gay. He then started taking us to clubs with guys dancing together and all that.

MICKEY: This strange man approaches you just like that?

SCOTT: I thought he was a con artist (*giggles*); we called the Better Business Bureau to check him out. We saw what he had to offer and he told us there were a lot of gays in it when we pose for photos, so that we had to get used to that. At that time I hadn't done anything sexually, though, and I didn't know that was part of the package.

Through the agent, I met Derek [Cruise] and we went out together and picked up people at both straight and gay clubs. We would take them home and have sex with them together. Last year I went to his wedding. I always wanted to do a scene with Derek. He never really made a pass at me, but we'd kiss each other when we were having sex with a girl. He's a little shy, though; even more shy than me, I think.

MICKEY: Derek is a great guy. You both have similar dispositions. You would have been great together in a scene. He married a very cool woman, got a good job and left the business. Did you suspect you were gay at the time you were first approached by the agent?

SCOTT: I had gay tendencies, but never did anything about it. In Virginia you couldn't do anything there, that's why I moved. (*He laughs*) I'd have to go to clubs in Washington, D.C., like Tracks, if I wanted to meet a guy. I had to keep it under the table.

MICKEY: You were in school at the time you were discovered?

SCOTT: I was in Virginia Tech College where I graduated—I have a double major studying business and human resource management—but out of school I was not making any money. I was finishing school and they gave me a call and asked if I wanted to do gay adult video.

MICKEY: Did you bring any of what you learned in college into the porn business?

SCOTT: My degrees helped me. Because after all, in this business I am dealing with people very closely, and I'm dealing with a lot of money that I should manage carefully.

MICKEY: When they called you, did you think a long time about it?

SCOTT: No, I said, "OK, I guess I can do that." They flew me out and there I was on the set and I hadn't done any of that before. Even going out with Derek, I hadn't done anything with a guy before. The first time was on video, it really was.

MICKEY: Have you seen yourself on video?

SCOTT: I haven't seen any of my videos. Not even **Flashpoint**! I don't think I'd like to see myself get fucked and stuff like that.

MICKEY: Why not?

SCOTT: It's strange. I was a virgin. The first time I sucked was on film. The first time I got fucked was on film. I wouldn't mind seeing it if I was topping, but not as a bottom.

MICKEY: Yet that's what people think of you as, a bottom.

SCOTT: But I've topped in video too, since the first time.

MICKEY: What do you prefer?

SCOTT: I'm versatile.

MICKEY: Do you consider yourself gay, hetero or bisexual?

SCOTT: Bisexual. When I'm with a lot of guys, I want a girl, and when I'm around a lot of girls I want a guy.

MICKEY: If you just wanted to have sex, who would you pick?

SCOTT: Both, if I can. When I'm on the road I like to have a man and a woman at the same time. I see a guy and ask him if he knows a girl and he goes to find one. It's especially good at clubs where they can see your body and are into you already. They don't like that at gay clubs. They don't like it when I do it.

But, I've had good experiences asking girls about doing three-ways, too. Girls don't seem to freak out when I say that I'd like them to go find a guy with a big cock. Girls like it. It's easier to do than you think, especially at straight clubs.

MICKEY: Before you got into the business, did you think you were bisexual or that you were attracted to guys at all?

SCOTT: As I grew up I noticed good looking men. I knew I was attracted to men. I would think, "He's not bad."

MICKEY: If you stayed in Virginia you'd be married with three kids by now.

SCOTT: (*Laughs*) No, no, no! Well, maybe.

MICKEY: Who do people say you look like?

SCOTT: People say I have a smile like Tony Danza. I'm Italian, I guess that's why we look alike—you know we all look alike. (*He smiles*)

MICKEY: Did you watch adult videos before you got into the industry? Either straight or gay?

SCOTT: Not a one. It was actually very scary the first time. I didn't know what to expect. The only thing I'd ever done before is streak in public with my fraternity. I worried about hard-on problems. I'm mean, being able to get one, but it didn't seem to be a problem, not at all.

I love showing off my body. I used to run in public naked all the time, so I'm an exhibitionist. I loved hanging out in front of my fraternity brothers.

MICKEY: Were any other frat brothers gay? Are all those stories true about kinky hazing activities and sex with the frat brothers?

SCOTT: You know, I didn't fool around with any frat brothers. But, one day, in my fraternity, I picked up a video and it was a gay adult video left behind by one of the guys, but I didn't think anything of it. We popped it in and then pulled it out right away. (*Laughs*)

We didn't think anyone in the fraternity was gay, though. That was impossible, no way. But now I wonder.

MICKEY: Would there have been discrimination in the frat if they found out, for example, about you?

SCOTT: If they found out, that would be bad. I never fooled around with a guy before I got in this business and I know that's kind of weird. But it would have been a definite no-no with the frat guys. I guess they'd beat you up and kick you out on your butt.

MICKEY: Do your friends know what you do?

SCOTT: I told one friend, another close friend knows I dance in gay clubs, and most of them know that I'm around gays a lot and am in gay magazines, but they're all pretty cool about it.

MICKEY: Does your family know?

SCOTT: They know I play gay clubs, but they think I do straight

In **Flashpoint**

adult films. They know I'm in gay magazines because people tell them they've seen me. They'd like to see me in real films.

They've seen some of my photos, but no nudes. They like the ones of me as a painter with half of my butt sticking out, the ones from Hot House. They thought that was a cute ad. They're real cool about it.

MICKEY: You do dance tours a lot, right?

SCOTT: I did 26 cities in two months, it's exhausting.

MICKEY: Doesn't your family run into your face being up on billboards all over the country, or in newspaper ads and in magazines?

SCOTT: Sometimes. My younger brother looks up to me and knows I dance in gay clubs, but my older brother is married and doesn't know too much about that life. I'm in the middle.

MICKEY: Do you ever want to direct a porn video?

SCOTT: I'm not really interested too much right now in behind-the - scenes or directing.

MICKEY: I've seen you out in clubs and when we've been at bars and restaurants together, and seen how people come up to you all the time. When you meet fans, what kind of questions do you get?

SCOTT: I get asked every question in the book. They ask what movies I'm in and why I got in the business. A lot of people are very shy to me, they're sweet and nonconfrontational. Most are not assholes of any sort. Nothing very negative has ever been said to my face.

MICKEY: You never get someone who's a bit inappropriate?

SCOTT: Some people don't like what I do, and they treat me a bit less than human. If people are negative I say, "To each his own" and I've said to a person before, "Hey, if you don't like it, it's none of your business." Then, they leave me alone for the most part.

MICKEY: What misconceptions do people have about you?

SCOTT: A lot of people think I'm an idiot. Maybe it's my Southern accent. I'm not stupid, I have my college degrees, and I like doing this.

MICKEY: What fantasy do you have that you'd like to do on video?

SCOTT: What I'd like to do is have a woman fuck me with a big strap-on. A lot of guys couldn't get into that, but I would. I don't think I'd want Sharon Kane to do it because to me, she's like someone who's so spiritual and wonderful, she's like a big sister to me. I don't know if I'd want Sharon to do that.

MICKEY: Is there something about the industry that you'd like to change if you could?

SCOTT: Everyone asks me if I make more money if a film does great, but I don't. And so, I think we should get residuals. **Flashpoint** is sold for $80 a tape and where is that money going? They pay us a thousand dollars or so, big deal. They're going to make millions off this video.

MICKEY: Do you have a type of guy you're most attracted to?

SCOTT: I like a dark guy, nice tan, Italian looking.

MICKEY: Like you a bit? What about dick size, is that important?

SCOTT: No, as long as it's a nice dick. I'm not that big, but I guess that it's the rest of the body that matters. I'm about seven inches, but people like me for my eyes, and I like that in other guys too. I like guys who can make love with their eyes.

MICKEY: What kind of sexual activity do you like best?

SCOTT: I prefer sucking and topping

MICKEY: Is there anything you want to say to fans of yours?

SCOTT: Yeah, I think so. People ask me, "If you're so smart then why are you doing this?" and I say, "I like this."When I dance I do seven shows a week, I make good money. I figure I might as well do it while I'm young. I have my whole life to sit behind a desk.

MICKEY: When you're at clubs has anyone ever come up to you and said, "You're straight and don't belong here?"

SCOTT: They have, once or twice. I like guys, I like having sex with guys. It's just time now that I start getting into a career where I'll have a bit of retirement. I'm leaving the business with no regrets.

MICKEY: So, if we see you at a desk job someday, we can say, "Hey aren't you Scott Baldwin?"

SCOTT: (*Smiles*) Yeah, as long as you tell me what your favorite scene was—sure that would be just fine with me.

The Bare Facts

Birthday: July 30, 1971
Zodiac Sign: Leo
Chinese Zodiac: Boar
Hair: Brown
Eyes: Emerald green
Height: 5-foot, 5 1/2-inches
Weight: 162 pounds
Cock Size: 7 inches
Favorite Color: Green
Born: Crystal City, Virginia
Resides: West Hollywood, Calif.
Workout Schedule: An hour a day every day

Mentor, *Vivid Man*
Nice & Hard, *HIS Interactive CD*
Officer and His Gentleman,
  Sierra Pacific
Our Trespasses, *All Worlds Video*
Prisoner of Love, *Vivid Man*
Santa Monica Place, *HIS Video*
Taste of Leather 2, *Catalina Video*
Total Corruption, *HIS Video*
Trickmaster, *Zack*
True Stories, *Hot House*
Uncut Club 5, *Rage Collection*
Virtual Viewer Photodisk,
  HIS Interactive CD

Videography

Backstage Pass, *Bullwhip*
Big River, *Falcon Studios*
Boys and Their Toys 2,
  Rage Collection
Center Spread, *Vivid Man*
Center Spread 2, *Vivid Man*
Cream of the Crop, *Catalina*
Cruise Control, *Catalina Video*
Double Vision, *Mustang*
A Few Fresh Men, *Studio 2000*
Flashpoint, *Falcon Studios*
Getting in Tight, *Forum*
Hold Me Again, *Jocks*
House Rules, *Falcon Studios*
Knight Gallery, *Vivid Man*
Man to Men, *Mustang*
Man's Touch, *HIS Interactive CD*
Manhattan Skyline,
  HIS Video Gold
Men of Forum 2, *Forum*

Photo courtesy: Hot House

True Stories: In The Classroom.

Jim Buck

"I've done jack-off shows before and I do them but I don't like to, in fact I don't stand up on stage. I get down in the audience and get them to interact with one another so that I'm not the only one performing, so to speak."

J im Buck seems like an old childhood buddy, who's just made it big, but remains as humble as ever. Did you ever imagine having a pal like Tom Sawyer when you were a boy? That's Jim Buck. Don't let his Southern accent and bayou simplicity fool you, he's a city slicker when he wants to be. Adept at the Internet, he's a computer geek with two earrings in his left ear, a light goatee and that famous Prince Albert which always has a stud through the head of it.

He's quite in love, now, and my boyfriend and I got to spend some time with his Jonno—another writer for a gay rag in Manhattan. They live together now.

Jim Buck first won Best Rising Star, chosen by the fans, at the Probies. At the *Gay Video Guide* Awards, his friend Vidkid Timo won Best Supporting Actor. Jim also won Best Actor for **Dr. Jerkoff and Mr. Hard** and Best Newcomer. At the 1998 Adult Video News Awards, Jim Buck picked up three of the top honors, Best Newcomer, Best Actor (this time for **Naked Highway** instead of his **Dr. Jerk-off and Mr. Hard** *Gay Video Guide* win), and Best Gay Performer of the Year. That puts him in second place to the most trophy winning gay pornstar in history (with Kurt Young still the reigning king).

He thinks people think he is "discombobulated," but he says he is, and that's OK.

He's also a chameleon. He can transform from a superstud raunch leather master to a naive virgin hick. This is the Everyman of Gay Porn.

MICKEY: You've started off pretty well in your career, and I'm glad that you took time off from your trip out here from New Orleans with your boyfriend to do this for the book.

Jim Buck

From **Dr. Jerkoff & Mr. Hard**

JIM: I'm delighted, although I think that I'm too new in the business to be in such a book.

MICKEY: There are others who have been in the business a shorter time than you; I tried to pick a diverse range of people. I've written and heard so much of you and director Wash West and was recently overwhelmed by **Naked Highway**. You did a great job and Wash seems like a nice guy.

JIM: He's really outstanding. He's outstanding to work with.

MICKEY: Yeah. You latched up with him pretty early in your career in porn, right?

JIM: Well I knew him in New Orleans. We moved in the same circles. We weren't exactly what I called the best of friends but we were certainly acquaintances.

And then after he learned that I was doing porn, after I had done a video, he actually helped us market it. We did it on our own in New Orleans. He helped us find the right company. Then he said, after watching it, "I liked your work, let's work together" and he's been one of my best friends ever since. He's really amazing and he's a great director and a great friend.

MICKEY: Had he directed his mainstream movie **Squishy Does Porno** at that point?

JIM: Yeah.

MICKEY: OK, I know he won a lot of accolades at the gay and lesbian film festivals all over for that.

JIM: Yeah. Yeah. As a matter of fact I met him during the final stages of **Squishy Does Porno** as it was being edited and hammered out and previewed in New Orleans.

MICKEY: What do you attribute to your connection with him?

JIM: Oh god. I was talking to my significant other just the other day about Wash and you know there are just certain people you meet who, it's impossible to dislike them. This is going to sound really biased but I think if you met him and sat down with him, you'd understand.

Anybody who doesn't like Wash, something is very wrong with that person. He's one of the most likable people you'll ever meet on the face of the planet. He's amazing. He's always cordial. He's always polite and democratic and really easy to work with. I know. I think that most actors who have worked with him find him to be that way.

MICKEY: Yes, that seems true.

JIM: He's very smart; he's got very clear ideas about what he wants to do with the script and he writes a beautiful script, by the way. He's really good with his visual and with his dialogue and putting a thing together. And then at the same time, just as he's got a very clear idea of where it's going, he allows for the production to become at least partly collaborative.

He's always open to ideas from the actors to say maybe the scene would go better if we did it like this. He's very open to that and I think that's good. I know a lot of theater directors who work better with just their clear vision and that's it, but maybe that's what makes Wash so really, really unique and easy to get along with. Because he's so completely wide open and laid back.

MICKEY: You have background in theater?

JIM: Yeah.

MICKEY: You have acting experience?

JIM: Yeah. I've been acting for, god, I guess since I was in the first grade—the first thing I ever did was in elementary school.

MICKEY: Do you remember what it was?

JIM: Yes, of course I do, because it was a momentous event. I went to this very silly private elementary school where every week at chapel each class would do a chapel presentation and they would be usually something like 20 minutes long and they were something silly about the history of the United States. One of us would dress up like Uncle Sam and the rest of us would dress up like a state or something like that.

This one time was different. My fourth grade teacher got it into her head that we were going to do something quite different. So, she found a production, she found a script for Hansel and Gretel, and it was in one of those *McCall's, Redbook, Good Housekeeping,* grocery store, point of purchase magazines and it ran about 45 minutes long. This to my mind was the longest chapel presentation they'd had before or since and I was Hansel and I remember getting such a complete thrill from that experience that I was hooked.

MICKEY: And the Best Gay Actor in a Porn Video was born! Did you do community theater?

JIM: I did community theater growing up and I did stuff in high school and debate and drama tournaments. My major was English but I had a Ford fellowship, which is a grant through the Ford foundation for undergraduates who are interested in teaching, as I am; it's sort of a directed study. You get to do a focused study in the area of your choice and mine was theater.

MICKEY: Wow.

JIM: It wasn't exactly a theater major but it was a study. Got my masters in Dramatic Lit and so, yeah, to make a short question a very long answer, yeah, I have a background in theater and I love it. I love it.

MICKEY: Great. Your connection with Vidkid Timo [**Mardi Gras Cowboy**] was really what got you into this, but as a younger person, before you got involved in it or knew about pornography, was there any fascination for you about it?

JIM: Oh I've been watching—I think I said this in my acceptance speech the other night but I'm not sure—but I really have been looking at porn and getting off on porn since I was a kid.

MICKEY: Really?

JIM: I mean, I've always been sexually precocious; I was a sexually precocious child from the age of 14. I mean, we would run across straight porn under our father's mattresses but then around 14 I started hanging out in public restrooms and hooking up with older men. Some of whom would meet me away from the public restrooms and a couple who were nice enough to give me their old gay porn mags, which were of course highly treasured by me. And so, yeah. I fell in love with Al Parker and that was it.

MICKEY: And did you think even at that age, "Gee I'd like to do that some time?"

JIM: No, not particularly. It was never really a driving ambition to go and do porn. It just sort of happened. I was at the gym working out and Timo said his lead had flaked and would I do it. I said, "Sure," without really thinking.

MICKEY: I guess the best thing to do is to not think about it too much.

JIM: I don't usually think about things too much when I make decisions. I sort of go with a gut instinct and then follow it. I figure it out later. That's actually served me really, really well.

MICKEY: Your trusting your feelings?

JIM: Yeah. For the most part there's certainly nothing that I regret. I really can't say that I have anything that I regret having done because even the stuff that didn't work out well I learned from. Like when I said "yes" to NYU [New York University] and went there, I'm glad I did it even if I didn't wind up staying at NYU. I was going for a doctorate.

MICKEY: Doctorate in literature?

JIM: No. That was actually in a very strange hybrid program that only NYU has. In a department called Performance Studies. It's sort of theater meets philosophy meets dance meets cultural criticism. Strange. The program, I thought, was going to be sort of the "be all/end all" of graduate school programs and it's a good program. It just wasn't for me. I said "yes" when I was accepted. I didn't even really think about any of the other acceptance letters that I had gotten. I said, "That's where I'm going." It didn't work out but I'm happy; that time that I spent in New

York was important to me.

MICKEY: Did you worry at all that doing this business might affect your teaching or your aspirations to teach?

JIM: You know it's funny. I had never considered that. I don't really think it will in the long run. Largely because I'm not too interested in teaching on an elementary or a secondary level. I am really more interested in teaching on the college level.

MICKEY: You went to school where?

JIM: I did my undergraduate in Mississippi. Then I did my masters in New Orleans and then I started my doctorate.

MICKEY: Was it a big school?

JIM: No, it's a very small little arts college that nobody will have heard of. It was a good education. It just didn't really prepare me for graduate school as much as it should have. But at least I learned how to think there. I didn't learn that from high school.

MICKEY: I'm sure a lot of fans have discovered you on the Internet. How are they reacting to you—are they asking "Is this really Jim Buck?"

JIM: Most of them actually get my e-mail address from publications like **Skinflicks**, that publish my e-mail address, so they know ahead of time. And mostly it's people writing, "Oh, I enjoy your work" and 9 out of 10 of them ask, "Oh, my god, I love your work, but didn't that hurt?"

MICKEY: I know what they're talking about!

JIM: Right. Talking about my Prince Albert and I have to explain. You know they want to know the basic questions of how I got into it and all that sort of stuff. I'm pretty good about responding. I'm pretty proud about my ability to hammer out responses.

MICKEY: Are you just pacing yourself with the number of videos you do?

JIM: I work with directors who I like working with and whose work I know and whose work I appreciate and so, yeah.

MICKEY: But now with the recent Best Actor award, you'll get recognized more and more. Tell me about what that was like getting this big first award. This is the first interview since you've won. How was that the other night?

JIM: Quite surprising. I mean really, really surprising. Especially the Best Actor. That came out of nowhere. I was flattered. I was stunned. I don't really know how to talk of it. It just sort of struck me as odd considering I'm not what I would consider the typical porn boy. I don't really have an amazing gym body. My looks aren't absolutely spectacular. I was up against some really really gorgeous men. I don't exactly know what the judges might have been smoking but I'm very happy they were smoking it.

MICKEY: Well I was one of them and I picked you.

JIM: Well, I was lucky enough to work on some really high profile stuff. **Dr. Jerkoff and Mr. Hard** was, from what I understand, a very popular video. It was widely promoted. **Mardi Gras Cowboy** got some good press. **Toolbox** did, too. Especially that final sequence is kind of notorious with Anthony Gallo and Tarik. It's one of my favorites.

MICKEY: And it seems like it's the boy-next-door quality that people are responding to; that's what both the fans and judges like.

JIM: That's the sort of niche I fill, I guess, in the desire department. Yeah. I guess so. I mean I don't fulfill the same sort of desire that Ken Ryker does or anybody of that stature.

MICKEY: Well I know it shocked a lot of people to see you in **Fallen Angel** for example. The little shaved look and all of that. That was your kinkiest, most fetishy video.

JIM: Right. That was fine. I enjoy that. That sort of stuff. I am open to everything and anything, I think.

MICKEY: Do you try to change your image? Role to role.

JIM: No. Not really. I usually do things like let my hair grow. Just because it can always be cut. It's the same way in theater. In general keep your hair long so that your director can shape it however he wants it. Apart from that, no.

MICKEY: When did you think that you had what it takes to do this? When did you realize that you had the gift for taking your clothes off in front of people, and that other guys liked your body?

JIM: I still can't compare to most boys or men in the industry, in that I'm not particularly well-endowed, but I'm really honest. I've been lucky enough to work with some very talented photographers who shoot me from very flattering angles. Michael, Mocha, Brian, all those guys. They're all really brilliant and they've got good eyes. But as for men, I figured out that people liked me or that I had some salable quality. I'm not really sure when. I guess it was when we started getting some reviews back for **Dr. Jerkoff** and the reviews were all very complimentary and certainly made me feel a boost. I'm a Leo so we need those every once in awhile. So I guess that's it.

MICKEY: Doing it the first time in front of the cameras, in front of other people, was there a particular mindset you had to get yourself into for having sex in front of people?

JIM: No. I didn't even think about it the first time. You know, like I said, I've been having sex in public places since I was a teen-ager. Whether it's a public restroom or a bathhouse, it was always in a public, one

Jim Buck

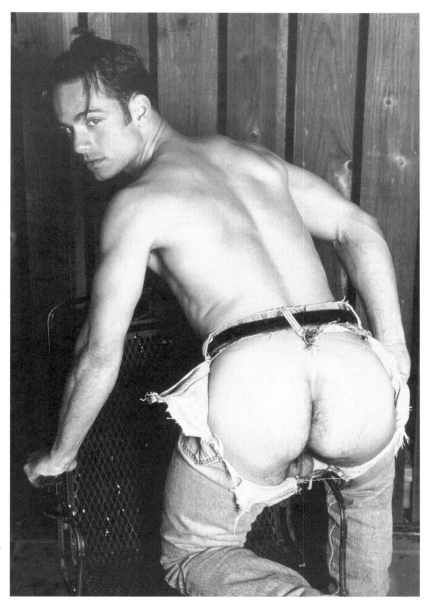

From **Dr. Jerkoff & Mr. Hard**

way or another.

MICKEY: You like being an exhibitionist?

JIM: I'm not really; I wouldn't really consider myself an exhibitionist. I've done jack-off shows before and I do them but I don't like to, in fact I don't stand up on stage. I get down in the audience and get them to interact with one another so that I'm not the only one performing, so to speak. I guess I'd be silly if I said I didn't like attention, because I do.

MICKEY: And obviously there are guys all over the country—and the world now—who we'll never meet, who are jacking off to you. What do you think of that?

JIM: I don't really have an opinion formed on that. That's Jim Buck who is separate from me, who's a character who only exists on video. Again I don't really think of the ramifications. It's just something that I did and it's happening somewhere. If they get enjoyment out of it, great ,but it's just one of many images available to them for fantasy.

MICKEY: Fans are always interested in relationships and how that works in porn. It obviously takes someone very special outside the business to deal with the fact that you are having sex with other people for work. Did your boyfriend Jonno know about Jim Buck when you were getting involved?

JIM: Yes. Yes, he did. It's funny because we met years and years before. Before I even thought about doing a film. But then when we re-met, it was at the wrap party for Chi Chi LaRue's **Hard Core.** It was in a specifically porn context in which we were re-introduced by a reviewer who knew exactly what I did so there was no question. He knew from the get go. It's not to say that it has been easy for him to accept. I think there are certain sorts of people who do porn. I mean obviously everybody is different, but I think that if there is one thing that most of us have in common, it is the ability to distinguish very clearly between sex and love or sex and something beyond sex that involves an emotional commitment or a physical emotion. However you want to phrase it, there is a threshold.

MICKEY: Yeah.

JIM: And it's probably very hard to accept, as a lover, someone who does porn if you can't make those distinctions yourself. I'm lucky my boyfriend can.

MICKEY: Do you want to say what you do in your real life?

JIM: I do a number of things; among them: I write. I'm a writer. There is other stuff obviously that I do. I help Timo produce his videos and market those. With all those factors going on, it is often very hard to get out here to do porn.

MICKEY: Is there a porn star whith whom you would like to work?

JIM: I think I guess I could say that I am very happy to have worked with the people whom I have worked with so far and I have never worked with anyone whom I disliked.

MICKEY: Do you have a favorite porn movie? Like the classics from your past that you just love or that always make you hard?

JIM: Oh god. Unfortunately my porn collection seems to get lent out. I don't see half of them, I'm lucky if I see too many of them ever again. I could go maybe by actor and say practically anything with Ted Matthews in it. Ted Matthews is gorgeous.

MICKEY: Yeah.

JIM: He's been around a lot and he's absolutely amazing. Anthony Gallo. Al Parker. My significant other has recently introduced me to the works of Lee Ryder who I enjoy quite a lot. Then just a lot of nameless hunks from the early Colt Films.

MICKEY: Do you have a type of guy who you like?

JIM: I'm lucky in that I find a range of people sexually attractive. Men, women, although by far I prefer men. I would hesitate to even call myself bisexual but there are women that are undeniably attractive. I mean, Sharon Kane is one of them, she's gorgeous and she's got that energy. That personality. But I can have a wide range of guys I'm attracted to. I find many, many, many different types of men attractive.

MICKEY: You're also from the younger generation of people who do not want to categorize themselves sexually. The bisexual label isn't completely accurate but they don't want to be pegged as gay or lesbian or hetero. It's like you're reflecting a trend in the world.

JIM: Right.

MICKEY: People are sexual no matter what.

JIM: Right. I hope that hits. I mean the problem with Western culture in general is our whole system is based in binaries. We learn things by learning in binary systems. Good, evil; right and wrong. Gay and straight. Inevitably, most things fall along the gray distance between the two. I think very rarely is anybody entirely straight and very rarely is anybody entirely gay.

MICKEY: But you identify as gay.

JIM: I think it's important to be gay for political reasons to really proclaim, yeah I'm absolutely gay. For political reasons. Like I certainly march in Gay Pride Marches and all that stuff because, don't get me wrong man, I love to sleep with men. But at the same time, in private, I am bisexual.

MICKEY: Do you watch porn at home?

JIM: I like just sitting at home watching porn. I love watching straight porn. Straight porn is a total turn on. It's my favorite.

MICKEY: Do you ever watch your own porn videos with your boyfriend as an arousal thing?

JIM: I don't think I could jack off to myself, but I do watch them. I've made few enough so that I actually know all the titles and have copies of them and all that stuff. So I do watch them but I don't usually watch them to get off. I'll sit through it with my boyfriend and we'll sort of take a look at the film as a whole and see how it works as a film. There are parts of my films that I enjoy watching.

Like there is that group scene in **Naked Highway** on the pool table that is amazing and totally hot, and there's the Anthony Gallo scene at the end of **Toolbox** that I enjoy very much. There are other scenes throughout that really get me off, but no, I can't watch *myself* to get off.

MICKEY: What would you change about porn? You are doing some changing already. What do you see as one of the things that you'd really like to see changed in either the way things are made or how they're done or the way the business works?

JIM: Well, I wouldn't say necessarily *change* because obviously there are certain types of porn. There are many different genres. Say there is Kristen Bjorn and his work, which is absolutely beautiful, and I can watch the Caribbean men in his videos a thousand times and it will still be the sexiest thing. There is quite a difference between their stuff and, say, **Naked Highway** and something like **Fallen Angel.** There are different types of sub genres within the genre of porn. I would like to see more of those sub genres. I think certainly some men just want to see hot guys getting off in beautiful surroundings. And then others like me who enjoy a little bit of thought with the movie. I think certain directors are doing that. Wash is certainly doing that. Timo's doing that. Timo's project may be, in the end, to create a new alternate porn genre that's more like an independent film with hard core sex scenes. So you get gay films but with hardcore sex and cum shots and things like that.

MICKEY: Do you have a work out schedule?

JIM: It's erratic.

MICKEY: Do you have a specific diet or just watch what you eat?

JIM: I eat—I live in New Orleans, the fattest city in the U.S. I'm constantly eating and it shows.

MICKEY: Are you from New Orleans?

JIM: Nearby.

MICKEY: Does your family know that you're doing adult videos?

JIM: No.

MICKEY: Do you think you'd ever tell them?

JIM: I don't know that I'd ever tell them; but if they know I think it will be fine.

MICKEY: OK. Anything you want to say to your fans out there or about the business or to people who think they might want to get into the business?

JIM: People who might want to get into the business: Make more amateur stuff. I'm really turned on by amateur video.

MICKEY: You know, so am I. I think it's one of the hottest things.

JIM: I totally get into amateur video and I think more people should be making it and marketing it.

MICKEY: And it's just like picking up a camera and doing it right?

JIM: Uh huh. There's nothing that turns me on as much. I'd prefer any of the men on the Internet. You know, the rest are scanned photographs from any number of magazines but what totally gets me hot is stuff like, it's somebody's personal home page.

MICKEY: It's great. I hope they never stop that.

JIM: I hope they don't either. I think eventually there will be some control put on it. The Internet. The Internet is a place for free speech and to watch your kids.

MICKEY: Would you ever want to direct?

JIM: I'd really feel more comfortable in the role of producer. Although, I'm not bad as a director. I just think there are other people that are much more talented than me at that.

MICKEY: You seem pretty happy these days.

JIM: It's been a good run. I've fallen haphazardly into every good situation in my life, most notably: jobs, degree programs, plays, porn, and, not least of all, my relationship with Jonno.

MICKEY: And how is that going?

JIM: Being in love is a very humbling experience. If there's one experience that can cause you to lose all sense of yourself, that forces you to put the needs of another before your own, it's probably love. If queers could get married, I'd say I was; as it is, I can only say that I'm emotionally, psychically, intellectually hitched to a significant other/domestic partner.

MICKEY: So, stop by again next time you're in town.

JIM: I will, I promise.

MICKEY: Y'all come back now, hear?

From **Dr. Jerkoff & Mr. Hard**

The Bare Facts

Birthday: August 19, 1968
Zodiac Sign: Leo
Chinese Zodiac: Monkey
Hair: Brown
Eyes: Hazel
Height: 5-foot, 10-inches
Weight: 160 pounds
Cock Size: 7 1/2 inches
Favorite Color: Plaid
Born: Jackson, Miss.
Resides: New Orleans, La.
Workout Schedule: Erratic.

Videography

1st Time Tryers, Vol. 2,
   All Worlds Video
Dr. Jerkoff & Mr. Hard,
   BIG Video
Fallen Angel, *Titan Media*
Gold Diggers, *All Worlds Video*
Hard Core, *All Worlds Video*
Mardi Gras Cowboy,
   All Worlds Video
Naked Highway, *BIG Video*
A Tale of Two Brothers,
   All Worlds Video
Toolbox, *BIG Video*

The two sides of **Dr. Jerkoff & Mr. Hard**

Derek Cameron

"I like sports: I like to water-ski, I like soccer, tennis, volleyball. I like football, I like to watch football. I guess I am a straight man trapped in a gay man's body."

Derek Cameron is so cute, he's like a teddy bear you want to sneak home and put on your shelf and take down and play with all the time. The soft-spoken stud and I first had dinner together just before he went off to the Italian countryside to film **Journey to Italy**, in which he plays a photographer who searches the breath-taking countryside looking for models, and gets caught in a whirlwind of self exploration and sexual awakening. He soon becomes obsessed with the handsome men he is photographing, and eventually gets into his work more than ever before.

Director Lukas Kazan, who comes from the part of Italy where they shot, says, "No one could be more perfect to represent the all-American guy than Derek Cameron. He is a joy to work with."

Derek was a huge hit at the Mi Sex convention, Europe's largest adult show business conference. He has also been featured in stories throughout Europe: in *La Republica*, Italy's large daily, and on the covers of *Adam,* and *Gay Italia.* Domestically, he made his splash in *Playgirl* in November 1995.

Since then, he's broken most of the stereotypes of porn. He's not a hustler, he loves to kiss, he's short, he's blond, he's got a pronounced Southern accent. He's also worked with some of the leading fashion photographers in the world: Dean Keefer, Tom Bianchi, Herb Ritts.

He flashes his picture-perfect smile as I go over to greet him at our favorite coffeehouse, The Abbey. It's a mecca in the heart of West Hollywood for gay pornstars who don't like the drinking crowds.

His green eyes sparkle as I hand him a tall shiny trophy, one of his last remaining lost trophies from a past *Adult Video News* award show.

Derek Cameron

Photos taken for **Journey To Italy**

He sports some beard growth, as if he's working on yet another look. He's a chameleon, sometimes hiding his earrings (on both ears), sometimes going for the rough look. Yet, it's hard for him not to look simply boyish and cuddly.

I'm drinking a double cafe latte and having a fat-free brownie which I offer to share. He waves his hand over it and says, "No thank you."

MICKEY: You probably don't eat brownies, do you? Even if they're fat-free?

DEREK: I'm conscious of what I eat, except during the holidays. I ate a lot when I went home to Texas. People say I look bigger but I don't know how I look bigger. I weigh the same. I do watch what I eat, though. I have to.

MICKEY: You're picking up a slew of awards this year—how does that feel?

DEREK: It was a real surprise for me this year, because I wasn't sure it was a good year. Everything I have done is not very highly publicized, except for maybe the **Journey to Italy** project, of course. I haven't done a movie-a-month, like a lot of people do. I take everything one step at a time.

MICKEY: What are you going to do with all these trophies?

DEREK: I'm serious, I'm going to have to go get a nice mantle to put them on. I've told my parents a little about it. They know that I won Best Erotic scene but I told them I was doing some independent film that would not get to their city.

MICKEY: One thing that I've admired you for is how you say you're not a hustler or circuit boy or porn stereotype.

DEREK: I also say that I'm a homosexual, not a fag. I'm very comfortable with my sexuality. I guess I live in the gay mecca but I don't come down and hang out a lot.

MICKEY: You won one of the biggest awards, Best Bottom!

DEREK: I was really surprised about that one and I turned totally beet red. It was the most embarrassing award to win. I kept thinking that's the award I hope I don't win.

MICKEY: Why not? What's there to be embarrassed about?

DEREK: It's a lot of pressure to live up to, to be Best Bottom—please.

MICKEY: You seemed very casual at the award shows. You seemed very comfortable up there on stage. Were you?

DEREK: That's good acting, then. I was really apprehensive about the awards this year. My agent did not want me to get my hopes up and

I didn't know what to say the first year that I won for Best Erotic Scene. This year I was as prepared as I could be. I had a date and it's nice to share an event like that with a close friend and go there and have someone to talk to and calm me down.

MICKEY: You seemed very gracious.

DEREK: People laughed because I had a speech written. After, though, people said I was great. That's nice. After the second intermission though, people weren't paying attention as much and I could hear everyone at the back bar, and I thought about saying, "Could you please quiet it down?" But, that's an awards show.

MICKEY: It was nice how you thanked people who you work with behind the scenes. Did anyone mention that to you after the show?

DEREK: I always think that's important. Whether they like you or not, there are a lot of people you have to work with behind the scenes and it's their job to make you look good, and I always try to treat them with respect and as friends. They're people to work with, too, just like the models, and you want them to work with you and like you.

MICKEY: Let's talk about Coy Dekker. He's one of the unsung heroes of the industry and a good agent and former star. He seems to be a very involved agent as far as you go.

DEREK: He is, and I think one of the biggest compliments [Coy's gotten] is he said director Jerry Douglas, who is an icon to the porn industry, said he saw some of Coy's directing work and was complimentary about it.

MICKEY: So you credit Coy with a lot?

DEREK: The reason I think I've been successful, if that's what it is, is because he and I talk openly. I made some mistakes without him, before I worked with him, like this billboard.

MICKEY: Oh yes, the cruise line billboard. You're all over town! Isn't that good for you as far as recognition goes?

DEREK: I'm also in Texas and New York, all over the world, and I didn't get paid shit for it. Whenever I'm seeing this big old billboard he's reminding me I could have gotten a lot more money for it. It's a gorgeous picture and people are constantly telling me, "I've seen you on the billboard."

MICKEY: It's a bit of a different look for you.

DEREK: Some people say I look very different. I change my looks about every six months and that's how you stay in the business and create longevity. If you do that, you don't get stereotyped. But everyone seems to like me looking younger.

MICKEY: You've also worked this year with one of the great icons of porn, Jeff Stryker, and it was real up-close-and-personal. How did that go? Was there any anticipation of meeting him?

DEREK: I still haven't seen that scene between he and I in **Jeff Stryker's Underground**. I'd love to see it.

It was really great and I like working with Jeff and I felt comfortable with him, even though I know he is *the* icon in the business.

MICKEY: That was a beautiful scene, where you play this innocent stable boy and he's on horseback and he says, "Come here" in his deep voice and you know he is just going to ravage you. Did you know how to ride horses?

DEREK: I love horses, but I didn't like those damn chaps.

MICKEY: And did you do anything special to prepare for him?

DEREK: I did some heavy breathing when taking up his dick.

MICKEY: Stryker told me that he hand-picked you as the model he wanted to work with in this scene.

DEREK: He didn't try to intimidate me and he treated me very much like an equal. I think he tried to make me as comfortable as possible. When we were together in makeup before the scene he was very nice.

After the shoot, he came to the pre-party for **Journey to Italy**. We had shot all day and everyone was kind of worn out and he came to that party afterward and that was nice. Unfortunately, I haven't gotten to run into him again, but whatever.

MICKEY: Did you have to prepare specifically to take Jeff Styker's huge cock anally? We all know that poor K.C. Hart was supposed to do a scene with Stryker sometime after your scene and wrecked himself up so much with a Jeff Stryker dildo that he couldn't do the scene. He tried to open himself up the night before the scene and ended up hurting himself.

DEREK: Yes, he damaged himself. I was a little nervous and K.C. Hart must have been a bit too anxious because Stryker isn't as big as his dildo. I almost made that mistake but the directors, John Travis [John Trennel on the credit of this video] and Gino Colbert, warned me to not take this cock-size thing out of proportion. Doing that bottom scene was nothing really unusual.

MICKEY: You look so boyish in that scene, you look like a little boy.

DEREK: I do. I think my hair was really a lot lighter and I liked playing the stable boy and being all innocent on the farm with the horses. I rode horses in Texas, and Jeff is a pretty good rider himself.

MICKEY: In another award-nominated scene, you're in that big orgy in **The Chosen**, and you're gang-raped by the hottest men on

Falcon's roster. What was that like?

DEREK: It was wild, it really was. Just watching Mike Branson fucking anyone is hot, but especially if it's me. I couldn't wait to get him in my mouth or in my ass.

MICKEY: Did director John Rutherford know what was going to happen?

DEREK: John Rutherford had known and it was really great when it happened. I had a lot of fun doing it.

MICKEY: Do you like to watch your own videos?

DEREK: Well, I'm comfortable. I know it's really me, I can watch it for my own enjoyment; and, sure, I know I'm watching myself. There is a differentiation.

MICKEY: Do you get off watching yourself?

DEREK: Oh, yeah, I'm remembering the moment.

MICKEY: And there's some grand moments, but some guys think that's weird.

DEREK: Oh, now, that's not weird. If I had a twin brother, we'd do each other all the time. I'd have no problems with it at all.

MICKEY: By the way, thank you for the postcards from Italy, keeping me up with what you're doing. I've quoted them a few times in my *Adult Video News* column.

DEREK: I know. I've seen it.

MICKEY: Tell us about working with these guys from Italy. Had any of them ever had gay sex in front of the camera before?

DEREK: One of them. The rest were all new to it, and I had so much on my mind trying to get ready to go over there I didn't really know what I expected. They knew I had done videos before and I knew how to get ready and how the shoot should go. There was one guy who was experienced and that's when I felt the most comfortable, and knew how to get his scene right. Some people like to work with new people and some people only like to work with professional people.

I felt like the old pro; I taught them how to relax. I felt like the captain of the team.

MICKEY: It was a great paid vacation, huh?

DEREK: It's a European vacation and work at the same time, and it got me out of the country for the first time. I had a lot of misperceptions. I wondered what it was like sucking on an uncut cock. I wondered if they had showers there, and I wondered if they had something other than goat's milk.

MICKEY: **Journey to Italy** was a beautifully romantic movie. Were you happy with it?

Photo courtesy: Men of Odyssey

A straight man caught in a gay man's body.

Derek Cameron

From **Journey to Italy**

DEREK: I think we really captured the romance. You don't see it much in videos, but romance is something we were shooting for, romance like no other video. We found locations in the countryside of Florence and Milan, villas and neighborhoods that never ever appeared in adult porn before, and probably never will again.

MICKEY: Is there something you'd like to do in a video that you haven't done yet?

DEREK: I'd like to do a water-ski type of movie, or jet ski, I just love water. Something like that. I would like to do something on the beach: I missed Falcon's **High Tide**.

MICKEY: Longtime veteran Dino DiMarco kind of got you started in this business, right?

DEREK: Dino DiMarco introduced me to agent Coy Dekker. Then I met Kurt Young, who was so great to work with in **Tradewinds**. We both won Best Erotic Scene for that in both big award shows. Matt Sterling takes his time doing a scene.

MICKEY: Who haven't you worked with whom you'd like to work with?

DEREK: I would like to work with Corey Evans, and Ion Davidov, from Bel Ami, one of the Czech guys. Then, the BIG Video guy who is exclusive, and his name is, uh, it is Clay Maverick, and of course Jake Andrews—I've never worked with him before. Of course there's Chris Champion, he's dreamy.

MICKEY: And your ultimate dream man to work with?

DEREK: My ultimate dream would be to work with Kristen Bjorn, especially after meeting him at last year's show.

MICKEY: How did these Italian men work out?

DEREK: I love Italian men, they're just so dreamy and hot. The guys there have these great blue eyes and wonderful skin; I find them very sexy. I didn't want to come back. I never slept with an Italian before this trip.

MICKEY: Would you like to direct a video someday?

DEREK: Maybe one day; it was a good experience working with new people. I feel like I could have my own idea and know what it takes to get it done and I think I can be firm. I would be a good director.

MICKEY: You don't seem the typical WeHo West Hollywood party boy at all—why are you living down here in the heart of it?

DEREK: I like it here. I run into all kinds of people. A lot of my friends are straight, however, and I don't go out all the time. I like soccer, tennis, volleyball, I like to water-ski. I like football, I like to watch it. I guess I am a straight man trapped in a gay man's body. I like to do straight guy stuff.

MICKEY: Do your straight friends know what you do for a living?

DEREK: Half of my friends know and half don't. I don't think it would make any difference to the half that don't, it just hasn't come up.

MICKEY: Are you dating anyone these days?

DEREK: No. I'm not dating anyone.

MICKEY: One thing I know is that you seem to like guys older than you, am I right?

DEREK: I like older guys, I identify with them. That doesn't mean a specific age range. For example, if I'm 26, then about 28 to 39 is how much older than me I like, but I've never really looked at that as much older. I want to be with someone I'm comfortable with. I need someone stable.

MICKEY: What do you think of the acting part of porn?

DEREK: The acting part is something that I want to do more of. I never had the acting bug or was interested in acting but hopefully in future developments I may do that in mainstream. I mean, I've performed as much as some soap opera stars, and the women in adult videos have done it.

MICKEY: Even though there's no secret that you're gay, women seem to respond to you very well.

DEREK: It was wild to see that in Italy. We were at a place called The Art Bar late last year and 1,000 people came to see me, and some people said they lived 2 1/2 hours away. It was about 50-50 men and women. The women said they loved me and some were waiting until 5:30 a.m. when I was leaving because they wanted to have my baby. I said, "Sorry, I'm too pooped!"

MICKEY: You have a Catholic background, right?

DEREK: Yes, my parents are divorced, and I have Czech, Irish, Swiss and German in my blood.

MICKEY: Tell me that great story about having sex in an airport bathroom that you told to *Playgirl*.

DEREK: I was with my boyfriend at the time, obviously, and we did it in stalls at the airport. He was a West Point cadet, tall, 5-foot-11, All-American, older than me. We broke up because of age differences.

MICKEY: Your family knows you're gay?

DEREK: My dad knows about it, and my mom; half my sisters took it well and half did not take my being gay well. I have four sisters, all older than me. When I was about 11 or 12 I used to jerk off with my nephews.

MICKEY: When did you realize how good looking you were?

DEREK: I never thought I was that good looking. I guess it was after winning the first award (at the *Gay Video Guide* Gay Erotic Video Awards) where I first realized how much I was noticed. Then, after the second win, it was super!

MICKEY: In school you were a swimmer, right?

DEREK: Yeah, that was hot for me. My mom was a lifeguard, and I could always check out the guys while they were sunning or in the showers. I knew I was attracted to guys and I think it was my underwater breathing techniques that helped me give better blowjobs.

MICKEY: Anything that you want to say to fans?

DEREK: God, I hope to make a lot of great movies and that people can identify with me and that I can live up to what people want to see of me.

The Bare Facts

Birthday: June 27, 1971
Zodiac Sign: Cancer
Chinese Zodiac: Boar
Hair: Blond
Eyes: Green
Height: 5-foot, 7-inches
Weight: 135 pounds
Cock Size: 7 1/2 inches
Favorite Color: Green
Born: Bay City, Texas
Resides: West Hollywood, Calif.
Workout Schedule: Two hours,
three to five days a week.

Videography

Big Chill, *Falcon Studios*
Centerfold Men, *Greenwood Cooper*
The Chosen, *Falcon Studios*
Heatwave, *Falcon Studios*
Jeff Stryker's Underground,
   HIS Video Gold
Journey to Italy, *Men of Odyssey*
Just Guys, *New Age Pictures*
Manhandlers, *Falcon Studios*
Manwatch, *New Age Pictures*
Morning Music, *Greenwood Cooper*
Red, White & Blue,
   New Age Pictures
Tradewinds, *HUGE Videos*

Photo courtesy: Derek Cameron

Signing autographs at MI/Sex in Italy 1997

Rex Chandler

"My cock looks larger because it's on me, but it's in proportion. I'm tall and thin. I don't look like I have anything but a big dick. But if you're only 5-foot-8 with that dick it looks like a monster."

Desperately trying to shed "Rex Chandler," this gentle giant keeps being haunted by his ubiquitous porn persona. He *is* Rex Chandler, no matter what mainstream movie roles he gets. He is also a prolific photographer in porn, and works with many of the other guys in these pages.

He's kind, he's funny, he's macho, he's sweet, and he's always swinging his big 10 incher. No blond god has ever had such a long-lasting impact on the porn industry, and guys still fantasize about him. I first got very friendly with Rex when he and his then-fiancé considered moving in downstairs at my Hollywood Hills home. The 6-foot, 5-inch man-mountain thinks nothing of hugging guys, and is always friendly. We've been on talk shows together, gone out to night clubs, and I've watched him as he handles his very wide variety of fans. He's single now, and I spent a great time in Las Vegas with him just before his jack-off and basketball solo video **One-on-One** from Paradox Pictures won Best Gay Solo Video at the *Adult Video News* Awards.

He had a good run off-Broadway, and I take partial credit for that. I was the one who told my playwright friend Ronnie Larsen that the role of the straight guy-turned-pornstar in his play **Making Porn** *was* Rex Chandler, and they took the play to Manhattan where it was a sold-out hit with Rex in the lead. He also won Most Outstanding Comeback at the first Probe Men in Video awards, voted on by porn fans throughout the world.

Now fully retired from porn, but still working in the gay adult world behind the scenes, Rex is focusing on breaking into the big time. He can be caught in a glimpse of Gregg Araki's **Doom Generation** as a

From **Rex Chandler: One On One**

murderous Nazi skinhead with fellow pornstar Zak Spears, who also uses his real name in the credits. He filmed a scene with Meryl Streep in **Death Becomes Her,** but it was cut, and he appears as himself in *Playgirl* centerfold Dirk Shafer's true comedy **Man of the Year**. He also appeared in **Raging Honor; Not a Love Story,** and earned a featured role in **The New WKRP in Cincinnati** on television after working with Sally Kirkland in her acting classes. As this is a porn book, I'm not giving you Rex's real name, because I don't want to mix up those two worlds for him any more than they are. If you want to find out, just look it up in one of these films.

Somewhat bitter about his lack of success in mainstream, his favorite slogan is "No Favor Ever Goes Unpunished." This Mr. USA (Michigan) in 1986 and Mr. Superman 1990 had invited porn rival Ryan Idol to his wedding and his stag party, but they had a falling-out and now have a not-so-polite rivalry.

Here's an inside look at the Golden Guy of Gay Porn.

MICKEY: Here I am, still writing about you—and you stopped doing videos in 1991.

REX: I guess I still carry a big name.

MICKEY: You did the solo tape recently and that's still a big seller, but could you ever be coaxed to do it with a guy again—on video, that is?

REX: No, probably not, but never say never.

MICKEY: I hear that a lot. How did you get into this business?

REX: It was a matter of deciding how to live my life and what I wanted and what I was able to do. So, it was decisions of how to get to where I was getting enough money to live the life I wanted. My manager and I were in Hawaii and orchestrated how to get a career going.

MICKEY: That was Mark Fredericks, who now has his own Studio?

REX: Yes. At first I was not thinking about what I was doing and that I was sticking my dick into someone's mouth or butt.

MICKEY: Was that tough the first time?

REX: The first time it was a nightmare. I couldn't get hard, and it took me four hours of doing it to make it believable. Suddenly it clicked and it wasn't so difficult anymore and I got hard.

MICKEY: You were talking about your slogan. Explain your slogan?

REX: My slogan is 'No favor ever goes unpunished.'

MICKEY: What does that mean?

REX: It comes from an Eastern philosopher named Deepak Chopra, who kind of mixes some of the new Western sciences with Eastern philosophy in life and all that. It basically says, "No debt in the universe ever goes unpaid."

MICKEY: OK, and?

REX: Well, in real time and in reality, like in life, no favor ever goes unpaid. I mean, if you can find one person other than your mother or father who will give you advice not shadowed by their own interest you're considered a lucky person.

So, most people—whether in business, acquaintances, friends, if you try to do something for them, you try to do them a favor, you are going to get punished for it.

MICKEY: And has that happened to you in the business?

REX: Of course it has, come on now. Working as a photographer (not as an actor) on the sets recently, this happens a lot where, you know, I've done some great work for some people and sell a lot of boxcovers and I ask for one simple thing: give me credit. Just put my name on the box. And it's not there. They tell me: "Oh, we forgot" or "I don't know who did that."

MICKEY: How did you and director Ed James get latched up when you were doing your solo video project?

REX: We didn't know each other really well up until recently, but we met seven years ago while we were filming **A View To A Thrill** in Hawaii. He was working as an assistant.

MICKEY: Tell us how the Rex Chandler dildo came about.

REX: Sitting in the car, bitching about certain things in the business and money and how—

MICKEY: How did you make it? Was it inspired by Jeff Stryker having a dildo?

REX: No, no, no. Not to take anything away from Jeff, it has nothing to do with that. It was more along the lines that it had been four or five years since I had really had anything out in this business.

MICKEY: You are still a strong force in the business, though; you are always recognized.

REX: There's a lot of things you can do and you don't have to still do movies. Someone said, "Do a fucking dildo. You're Rex Chandler. I mean you don't have to do anything. Put out the dildo, take the pictures, and sell it." You know what I mean?

MICKEY: But you didn't do that right away?

REX: I thought about it. And then I said, "Let's do it." I'm not kidding, for two or three months Edward James busted his ass making the deal. And I mean back and forth with a lot of people, and we test-marketed it first. We called up some people in Australia, we called up some people in Germany, and we called some people in Russia. The guy in Australia said, "Well, that man hasn't had anything out in years, but anything he puts his name on we'll buy."

MICKEY: Wow!

REX: It's a good product that we worked really hard on with the pictures and the video.

MICKEY: Why did you decide to come back into the business? I mean, you had retired, although I guess the mainstream stuff just wasn't working that well.

REX: No, it's not that. But it's not that I was turning down roles in the mainstream business either. When I say I left the business, I left hardcore, OK? I don't know if I'll ever leave porn.

MICKEY: Right.

REX: I retired from doing hardcore. I'm not doing that anymore. But as far as the community and the business, I imagine that no matter what I'm doing or what movie I'm involved with in the future in mainstream, I'm always going to be involved in this somehow. Always.

MICKEY: What charities are you involved with now?

REX: Aid for AIDS. We had to get their permission to put that on the box of the dildos and the video.

MICKEY: It's nice to know you're still involved in charity causes, and it's interesting that the charity is involved in a dildo.

REX: Obviously making money is a big motivator. I'm not going to deny that. But at the same time I think we're giving a fair product. It was real important to me how the box was constructed, the pictures that went on it.

MICKEY: Then, you bared all again in the solo video. You jerk off three times in the movie, play basketball, go to the beach, work out in the gym.

REX: The biggest difference is that most solo videos are boring. They are. I don't care how beautiful the man is—you watch it, they're boring. And, they're shot in one day or two days. We worked on this **Rex Chandler, One on One** for six weeks.

MICKEY: Why did it take so long?

REX: We used several different locations. A lot of it is MTV style, so it's a montage and not real boring. The basketball, at the beach, stretching, working out, art stuff and whatever. And three different cum shots that show different areas and places. And there's no speaking in it, no words.

MICKEY: Does this mean you're not going to be doing sex scenes anymore—we can't even persuade you to do one?

REX: I will not do any more hardcore scenes. If I do anything with

Rex Chandler

In **Idle Pleasures**

other actors on camera with me it might be something like doing a wrestling video, a pump video, and things like that.

MICKEY: Has being in the adult industry shut doors of opportunity for other parts of your life?

REX: I've had as many doors shut as I've had open. I understand that. We have enought of our own money to make these soft-core productions, little T&A movies, the stuff that sells on cable, to be able to shoot 35 mm.

MICKEY: Are you going to do your own mainstream movies?

REX: Maybe someday. I have some ideas. I'll do softcore. When I say softcore, no hardcore sex is what I mean. Nudity yes, a tease.

MICKEY: You've had some pretty impressive acting training?

REX: I worked with Sally Kirkland and acting coach Stella Adler, and I learned the method stuff. They always wanted you to explain why you got into things. I am like a light switch—I could turn it on.

MICKEY: Back to how you did the dildo.

REX: It was very difficult.

MICKEY: Every vein is actual?

REX: Yes, the veins are actual. It's very true to life. I'm tall and almost 230 pounds. I don't look like I have anything but a big dick compared to someone who's 5-foot 8-inches. My cock looks larger because it's on me, but it's in proportion. I'm tall and thin. I don't look like I have anything but a big dick just standing there. But if you're only 5-foot-8 with that dick it looks like a monster. A lot of people came up to see it when I was molding it.

MICKEY: So you had quite an audience while you were getting your dick hard for the dildo mold?

REX: That's right. What was funny is that the guy had a little sketch pad and was circling around me and drawing everything in, and they took a photo of everything. The process was amazing. They also videotaped it in case anyone was to say, "Oh, that didn't really come from him." We had to have some proof.

MICKEY: How was the female fluffer? I heard about that!

REX: Oh my god! Whatever it would take to keep it going. She walks by, and all of the sudden she shut the lights off. And then 10 power strokes from her, man—boom! God, I felt like I was 15 again! She walks by, wipes her face off; she had just taken a sip of coffee. She goes, "How did it go?" She said, "Oh, he came good."

MICKEY: I see you didn't add to the balls thing like some others did.

REX: You know the stores set the price to pretty much what they want. They have the lee-way to double or triple the price. It's unbelievable. So, when you start adding things like revolving balls—which is a good idea—when you start doing that, though, you start upping the distribution price and it costs everybody more money.

MICKEY: How did this all come about?

REX: A company came to us while I was moving and going through a divorce, and he tells me they're interested in doing this. I got a deal and we have our own in-house manufacturer. This guy is a hustler. He works really hard.

MICKEY: He's the one who actually does all the casting?

REX: Yes, he is. He does everything.

MICKEY: Incredible!

REX: I worked to get the word out, too. Every place around the country, and in Montreal—you name it, I did it. I worked my ass off. You want to talk about no favor going unpunished? Working with all those public appearances was tough.

MICKEY: When did you realize your marketability? When did you realize, "I am a big name in this business?"

REX: It was in Florida. I was dancing with this group of guys at the Warsaw Club.

MICKEY: So they know you all over the country still?

REX: Yes. This one guy named Albert, with long hair, really good-looking guy, great dancer, lent me his 5.0 Mustang and I was told to show up at the Warsaw at 1:00 in the morning. That's when the show was going on. I pulled up and I saw what I thought was a riot. I had never seen anything like that before. You know what I mean? It was amazing.

The line was at least seven blocks long. Seven city blocks long. Posters of me all over the city of Miami. I pull up and this cop says, "Hey buddy, you can't park here." I said "Hi, I'm Rex Chandler, I'm—", "Oh, pull in right over here." I get in, I literally ducked in. People tried to touch me. It was 30 percent women in the audience. They saw the posters, that's what it was. Then I was standing on stage in my underwear in front of over 3,700 people.

MICKEY: Wow!

REX: With a microphone handed to me, I was in control. It was complete silence when I spoke. They had respect, and after the show I was doing a question-and-answer session and it was such a high. That's when it hit me.

MICKEY: Did you give 'em a good show?

REX: Yes. I was amazed. Literally amazed. We did a little sexual, risqué act.

MICKEY: That's actually after some of your bigger videos, right?

REX: Yeah, right during it. The sexual, risqué theater act that we did got a lot of notoriety, dancing with handcuffs, whipped cream, it was a lot of fun. It was really a well acted thing. It was a good time. It was probably one of my favorite touring experiences; that and Montreal. It was a blast.

MICKEY: What do you think of the other large cocks in the business?

REX: Where is it written down that 9 1/2 inches is a standard for being hung? I mean, everybody here is 9 to 9 1/2 inches. That's what they say anyway. It's bullshit.

MICKEY: Well, it depends on how you measure it.

REX: Exactly. If you measure it from the asshole, around the back side, then maybe you're 9 1/2, then everybody is.

MICKEY: When did you realize that you had something unusually large?

REX: When I was 16. I met this woman named Renee. Her father was a bigwig in the Ronald Reagan I-Can Corporation. She had lots of money and she was older than me. She was 24 at the time but she looked like Sophia Loren. Very red hair and glamorous. I was under age and met her in a bar. I wanted to take her to my senior prom! No, I was 16, so my junior prom! She whispered in my ear, "How would you like to pick up a bottle of Schnapps and go for a country drive?"

Oh my god! It was a '79 Cutlass with leather seats. After we fucked once, with her riding on top of me, I decide to go outside and take a piss. It was freezing cold (I grew up in Michigan), and I'm trying to piss and I've got drippy cum dick and I'm trying to piss out of it. You know how your piss goes in five different directions trying to get it out. I know I've got someone waiting in the car, and I'm pee shy as it is, I'm a freak when it comes to that. Anyway, I go back in and you know you've got that staying power the second time around when you can get it up again after that.

MICKEY: Yeah.

REX: She was talking to me a lot, like "Bang me, cum in me" whatever it was. I remember she said something to me like "You're really hung" and I said, "Really?" It said something to me. But let me tell you something: Women really lie about dick size more than men.

MICKEY: Like they say they don't really care about it?

REX: Yeah, they lie about not caring, but men are fucking honest. Men are brutal about it. But women are cruel when they talk to their girlfriends behind your back and shit. Oh my god! They are vicious. She broke my heart.

MICKEY: Is there anything you want to say about the business, or about fans?

REX: I look at it like this. It's hard for me to be in the other chair, to think of idolizing somebody like myself, or wanting me in that way, but I think this dildo of me is a cool way for someone to buy something that literally is the same shape, the same size, as me. That's me, the whole bit and anyone can have fun with it sexually.

MICKEY: So is it a turn-on for you to know that there are going to be guys and girls all over the world using this?

REX: Oh, definitely. Of course it's an ego trip. Its a turn-on. It makes me happy. It's one more thing that boosts my ego. So look, you know I'm not going to be President of the United States.

The thing is this, life is like this: you blink one second, you're gone. You're gone. I just try to do as much as I can. I have a philosophy. I didn't create it, but I follow it: Do as much as you can do with your life. Do as much as you can do to get ahead, just don't hurt other people doing it. That's the whole thing. Just try not to hurt anybody else.

MICKEY: That sounds nice. You did a Donahue Show with our mutual friend *Playgirl* centerfold Dirk Shafer? That was more exciting than some of the local talk shows we've done together.

REX: (*Laughs*) Yeah, we did Phil Donahue just before he went off the air, it was one of his last shows. Our moms went on with us and it was a very popular show.

MICKEY: You talked about how you kept it a secret and how you got started.

REX: She didn't know any of it. She didn't know how director and photographer Mark Fredericks found me in Ohio where I grew up—we had a mutual friend whom I worked for in Ohio, and anyway, he wanted to do some greeting cards with me that were semi-nude. So, I was young and I was broke and just 21 and that's what we did.

MICKEY: You get some flak about saying you're straight still, don't you?

REX: I treat everyone with the same respect as I expect for myself. And as far as the sexuality, I always know that there's going to be a certain number of people who are going to be resentful about it. I don't care if they say, "I know he's bisexual" or "I know this or that." That's fine; I've always respected people's questions. Always. I hope that people respect my answers.

MICKEY: Ultimately, you want to go into mainstream, right?

REX: Ultimately, I want to act, of course. I really want to perform, regardless of what I do behind the camera, because I love working with photography, directing. I want to act!

I would love to wake up every morning and not have to worry about a goddamned thing except for my roles, working out, being in shape, and getting in character. That's ultimately what I want to do, and one of the things we are doing with these products we're putting out. In the solo video, it's still me.

MICKEY: No matter if it's your real name or Rex Chandler on the product?

REX: Right. I add something different to this industry. I'm trying to show people out there that regardless of whatever the format is, whether it's adult film, whether it's the solo video or the dildo, it's me and I'm different. I put something different into it. And I'm trying to expand into mainstream, and I hope all the people in adult films will continue to support me in my endeavors in trying to make it to the silver screen. People out there are going to read this; they know.

The Bare Facts

Birthday: August 14, 1966
Zodiac Sign: Leo
Chinese Zodiac: Horse
Hair: Blond
Eyes: Blue
Height: 6-foot, 5-inches
Weight: 230 pounds
Cock Size: 10 inches
Favorite Color: Deep blue
Born: Mount Clemens, Mich.
Resides: Hollywood, Calif.
Workout Schedule: One hour, two times a week.

Videography

Chi Chi LaRue's Screwing Screw Ups, *Pleasure*
Cocktails, *Catalina Video*
Deep in Hot Water, *Catalina Video*
GV Guide All Star Softball Game #1, *Greenwood Cooper*
Heat in the Night, *HUGE Video*
Idle Pleasures, *Catalina Video*
Made for You, *HUGE Video*
Man-Rammer, A Battle of Size, *Falcon Studios*
Men With Big Toys, *HUGE Video*
Rex Chandler: One on One, *Paradox Pictures*
Rex Take One, *Catalina Video*
View to a Thrill 2: Man With the Golden Rod, *Planet Group*

Being interviewed at the *Gay Erotic Video Guide Awards* by Nicholas Snow, the Tinseltown Queer.

Will Clark

"People are always asking me, "Isn't it humiliating?" I'm like, let's see, they are paying me a nice little chunk of change to fuck or be fucked by really, really good-looking guys. Try to find the humiliating thing in that sentence."

He's a red-head, and when I first met him I told him that redheads don't usually make it in porn. Boy, was I wrong! Will Clark took the industry by storm as a dependable, lovable, nasty performer. He co-hosted the second Probe Men in Video Awards show, picked by the fans, and was given Best Bushwhacking by the fans for the most creative pubic hair trim. He loved it.

Will is one of the first to dive in for any AIDS benefit or good cause, and has stripped and danced for free. He's also a favorite nude bartender at the raunchy A-Men Bulletin Board parties in West Hollywood, where he says, "I make the drinks stiffer as I strip down and the tips get bigger!" That's why he was a nominee for Best Humanitarian at the *Gay Video Guide* Awards in 1997.

After his major hit, **Night Walk**—he was in one of its hottest scenes with Dino DiMarco—this handsome buffed stud has a fan club, and every guy wanting to meet him. He is very popular on the Internet and responds to messages promptly. He is now with a boyfriend who may even get into porn someday himself.

We are at Basix Cafe, on Santa Monica Boulevard in West Hollywood, one of his favorite spots.

MICKEY: So, how did you get discovered?

WILL: I wasn't discovered. I was living in New York, dancing at clubs for fun and a little extra money.

MICKEY: What clubs?

WILL: The Palladium and Limelight.

MICKEY: So these weren't jack-off clubs?

WILL: No, these were stand-up-on-a-box and be a go-go boy kind of

The guy-next-door red-head in **Take It Deep**

clubs. I was having a really great time doing that and I was getting a few more bookings. I was pursuing a career in acting and hadn't been really happy with it because the whole professional attitude is just not fun. I was in a show, a real sort of campy show where I played a drag queen and I got to strip at one point because it's revealed that I'm really a butch kind of vice cop. It's really scary. I'm like the ugliest woman on the planet. Real scary.

MICKEY: So do you strip totally?

WILL: No, down to some tiny sort of Speed-o thing.

MICKEY: What was the show called?

WILL: It was called **The Lascivious Transformation of Mr. X.**

MICKEY: Were you Mr. X?

WILL: No, Mr. X was this sort of hunky beefcake straight boy who plays this sort of Jekyll and Hyde character.

MICKEY: Does he turn gay?

WILL: Well, he's sort of tri-sexual; he'll *try* anything. He'll fuck sheep, men, women, everything. He does it offstage with about three different characters during the course of the show.

MICKEY: Was this an off-off Broadway show?

WILL: It was an off-off-off Broadway kind of thing. It was one of those things where it was really funny if you go see it at 11 or 12 o'clock at night if you're punchy and a little drunk or whatever. It was like a **Rocky Horror** type of thing.

MICKEY: It sounds like it.

WILL: While I was doing that show I started working for an escort agency, and that started to propel me into more of the sexual sphere.

I asked a friend: "Do you know anybody in California I could talk to about doing movies?" He said, "Oh, yeah!" and started writing down names of people. So when I got out here I just called a couple of people just out of curiosity to see if I could handle it, if they were interested. It was something I really wanted to enter into, so I guess I wasn't ever discovered, I just looked for it myself.

MICKEY: That's actually an unusual way of getting into it.

WILL: Oh, really?

MICKEY: Yeah. It's usually if Chi Chi LaRue sees someone dancing in a club, it's sort of, "I'm going to put you in a movie."

WILL: Well, I've heard that from a lot of models I've worked with so far "Chi Chi found me" or "This company or that company found me dancing on a box at a club in D.C." or this place or that place. Part of me kind of regrets that I didn't get discovered.

MICKEY: Why porn?

WILL: Why not? I don't know. Probably one of those complex, psychological, self-esteem, narcissistic things, sort of, "Oh, am I that good-looking that people will pay me to have sex" or pay to see a movie that I'm in, or be all that interested. That's half of it. The other half is that I thought it would be kind of fun, and why not?

MICKEY: It seems like there's usually one of three reasons that people get into it. What I've discovered in all the interviews I've done is they're either exhibitionists and want to take their clothes off in front of people, they need the quick money, or they want to get paid to fuck really good-looking guys.

WILL: People are always asking me, "Isn't it humiliating?" I'm like, lets see, they are paying me a nice little chunk of change to fuck or be fucked by really, really good-looking guys. Try to find the humiliating thing in that sentence. I can't figure it out yet.

MICKEY: Right. Exactly.

WILL: This has sort of become my paradigm in that people will always say, "Isn't that humiliating?" I say going to an audition, and spending $100 for 100 head shots is humiliating, and then sending them to 100 companies and not getting one call, that's humiliating. Or going to a temp job and having them treat you like shit, that's humiliating. Doing catering or waitering and having them call you the hired help, like if you're at someone's private home and they say, "Oh, that's just the help." That's humiliating. So I don't think that escorting or doing porn is at all humiliating in comparison.

MICKEY: That's a really good point.

WILL: There really hasn't been a moment that I can recall that I was treated really badly, when someone degraded me, or made me feel that I was a jerk, or new, or stupid. If anything, everybody's been very gracious and very nice. People keep saying it's a horrible business but I keep waiting for it to be horrible. I know there's a drug underbelly to it, which I'm not interested in getting into, but it's easy enough to avoid.

MICKEY: You've never seen it on the sets, right?

WILL: Once. But that was not necessarily sanctioned by the studio. It was a specific situation.

MICKEY: The 40 or 50 sets that I've been on, I've never seen drugs yet. If someone comes in stoned, they get sent home.

WILL: People also told me, "There's all these drugs and they'll force you to do them." And I'm like, "How are they going to force me to do them, stick it up my nose?"

I can't get it up if I'm drinking or high. The function just doesn't go there. That's a biological fact. For me anyway. Maybe for some people it really heightens it. You pump something into me and I'm useless. It's good for dancing maybe, but it's not good for having sex.

MICKEY: Were there faulty perceptions about the business that you had personally?

WILL: Sure. I'm from the Midwest.

MICKEY: What part?

WILL: Wisconsin. A beautiful small little town of about 3,000 people. It kills me—I mean, there were 3,000 people on my block in New York.

You know the perceptions are that it's really humiliating, or it's evil and horrible and the people that are in it are in a dead end world. They have no other choice but to do this. It's some of the same misperceptions people have about being gay.

People say stuff like that to me all the time: "There's no future, there's no hope, you're the faggot that's going to bump himself off in the end like in the movies." That doesn't seem to be the case at all. There are a lot of people involved in the industry who are quite sane and highly intelligent and accomplished.

They are either doing it because they think it's fun and a kick, or they rejected some other areas of the performing arts for various reasons, as I did. I think the day that I had to suck off the director to get a role in a show was the day that I said, "What's the difference between this and doing porn?"

MICKEY: The casting couch?

WILL: It only occurred last year—and it was for a bad show, too. It wasn't for a really big Broadway show. It was just this little show.

MICKEY: I hope it was a straight director, too.

WILL: No, no. That would be cool. That would have made it worthwhile.

MICKEY: That's shitty.

WILL: It was not like he came out and said: "if you suck my dick I'll give you the role." It was more implied.

MICKEY: Did you get the role?

WILL: Yeah, but I turned it down. I realized I didn't want it under those circumstances.

MICKEY: Did you realize there was this much acting involved in pornos?

WILL: Oh yeah, I was hoping there was. It would be really boring to just go in there and fuck and then leave, you know. You'll see that in **Night Walk**. I played Dino DiMarco's faithful butler, kind of like Batman and Robin, and I'm always around lurking in the shadows. Actually, [director] Gino Colbert hired me because I had an acting background. I told him I majored in theater; I have a Master's degree in Theater.

MICKEY: Did you do any auditions?

WILL: No, actually the agent I had at the time knew Gino and called him over and showed me a couple of trailers from **Latex,** the first, straight version of **Night Walk**. I had never seen anything quite like that before. It blew me away! Now that I think about it, he did give me a script and we went through it. Then he said, "Go into the next room and strip and when you're ready we'll take a picture of you."

Just the thought of it made me instantly erect of course, even before I had taken off my clothes. Then I said, "OK, I'm ready," and they're like "Jesus Christ, already?"

MICKEY: So that was a turn-on.

WILL: They were just amazed and I said, "What's wrong, did I take too long?" They said "No, usually we have to wait 20 minutes before anybody can get it up."

Like anything, if you can do it fast and quick, there's a product.

That's what a majority of the industry is for reasons of economics. They have only enough time, only enough videotape, that's just how it's set up. Like soap operas. You do a soap opera real fast—you have to do everything on the first or second take because you don't have time to wait. That's why I use this analogy. It's because you have to get the product out fast, fast, fast.

A lot of people don't respect the soap actors, they don't respect that medium either. There are so many similarities, when you think about it, between soaps and porn.

MICKEY: Had you watched porn movies before? Were you a fan of them?

WILL: No, I didn't really know anything about them. I'm like the soap star actor who gets hired and says "I've never watched the show. I have no idea who these characters are." I watched maybe a couple of movies in my life, and not even all the way through.

MICKEY: You were a fast-forwarder?

WILL: I just wasn't interested. Somebody would have it on and I would watch it.

MICKEY: Did you know that people you worked with like Chance Caldwell were big names in the business?

WILL: No. I think in a way that was good. If somebody was physically imposing, big, or strikingly beautiful I sort of took my cues of "Wow." Like I said before, I'm nice and respectful to everybody. I don't know who I'm dealing with on any level. I don't know if the director I'm working with is 'A' list or 'D' list. I'm the same way with actors, or studios, really.

Other than Falcon, and only because it has such a reputation in the gay world, you know that. You just know that Falcon is the biggest maker of gay porn. And Colt Studios, I guess. But Falcon really is the big thing.

I think I've taken some interesting turns along the way and worked with some people that my agent wishes that I hadn't done work for.

MICKEY: So you have had an agent representing you?

WILL: Yes.

MICKEY: Does your family back in Wisconsin know what you do?

WILL: No. They think I'm doing theater work, that's what they know about. The money I make from both will enable me to do my writing. When I approached this I said "OK, if I'm going to really do this, I'm going to do it right." The money should be invested. I should take some out for living expenses, and that's cool. But I don't think I need to take a trip to Hawaii, or buy a new car or all new clothes. I'll invest this for the future. I'm only going to be young and beautiful for a couple of years.

MICKEY: Do you have a philosophy of life that you follow?

WILL: Yes, I'm realistic: "Don't be foolish enough to think that this is going to be forever. Start preparing now for when this is over." I'm continuing my writing. I'm using some of the money to write new plays, and to get the play I have written published and to a Broadway type of level. I'm not going to lose sight of the overall goal. This is the way I'm making money now. It'll be fun and great. I'll have a little library of films. I take it very seriously, but it's not forever.

MICKEY: Did you every consider that this could haunt you?

WILL: I think it could haunt me more if I was going to go into politics, which I wouldn't do.

MICKEY: Do you consider yourself to be an exhibitionist?

WILL: I really dance along that edge a lot. Because sometimes it is such a turn-on but sometimes I just get horribly embarrassed and scared, like, "Oh my god, what if I don't have anything they want to see" or "Oh my god, I can't get erect."

MICKEY: Has anyone asked you for autographs yet?

WILL: Gino called me and said, "I've got a friend who is in New York who would like to see you do a private photo session." And I said, "Sure." When I got there he said, "Would you sign my magazine?" I went, "Wow! This is so bizarre!"

MICKEY: And it's only going to get worse—or better, or whatever.

WILL: People say "That happens all the time." When it happens to me, I feel like an 8-year-old school girl again.

MICKEY: It's very refreshing that you have that kind of attitude because you don't hear that from people. A lot of people come into the

Clockwise from top left: Outdoors (1996), Gay Pride with Kurt Young and Dino Phillips (1997), Hollywood Hills (1996), from **Making The Team**.

business jaded already.

WILL: You have to have a sense of humor about it. If you're not going to have fun, why bother? I'm not going to do anything if it's not going to be fun. Work can be fun, and should be, I think.

MICKEY: Even in mainstream acting there are very few actors that are redheads. This is especially so in the porn industry.

WILL: Actually, one company wasn't interested in me because I was a redhead. They just said "You're a redhead, we can't use you." I'm not just the color of my hair.

MICKEY: But you've got to prove to them that you can do it.

WILL: When I was growing up, I really hated having red hair. I was different from everybody else. I got teased a lot, and I really hated it. I always dreamed of having black hair. I realized later that those were the guys I was really attracted to. I wasn't able to formulate that at 8 years old. Those were the guys I thought were really attractive.

MICKEY: I was going to ask you if you have a type of guy that you are really attracted to.

WILL: Well, hairy or not, that's not really an issue. Size is not an issue with me. Muscular, dark hair.

MICKEY: About your height?

WILL: My height or taller. I like strong. The Blue Blake look that is very big, I really like that.

MICKEY: That's a bit like your boyfriend now!

WILL: He's really got an incredible body. He's also one of the sweetest people.

MICKEY: What sign are you?

WILL: Pisces. I swing two ways!

MICKEY: Does that make you bisexual?

WILL: No, I'm not.

MICKEY: Do you have a workout schedule? Do you workout regularly?

WILL: Yes, I work out. But my workout schedule has been a bit less lately because I have tennis elbow right now. So during the last month I haven't been working out as much as I used to, but usually it's four times a week.

MICKEY: Do you play tennis?

WILL: No, I don't. I work out, I like to bicycle. I like to take walks in the park. I love to travel. Get me on a plane and take me somewhere and I'll be so happy. And being by the ocean. I don't tan by the ocean because my skin is so fair. But I love walking along the ocean, like down by Laguna Beach. That little stretch is my slice of heaven on the planet.

MICKEY: Do you have any brothers and sisters?
WILL: One of each.
MICKEY: Are you in the middle?
WILL: At the end.
MICKEY: So you're the youngest?
WILL: I'm the youngest.
MICKEY: Are any of the others gay?
WILL: Nope. My brother is exceptionally homophobic. Does that sort of count?
MICKEY: That's not good.
WILL: He hasn't spoken to me in seven years!
MICKEY: And he doesn't even know what you're doing.
WILL: No. Just the fact that I'm gay is enough.
MICKEY: So you are out to your family?
WILL: Oh, yeah. They know, but we don't really talk about it. It's a Midwestern thing. You don't really talk about sex in any way. When I was growing up though, my Mom and Dad were very affectionate. You know, kissy-kissy, touchy-feely with each other. So it was a very nice role model. But we've never actually talked about sex.

And they've certainly never talked like, "Do you have a boyfriend? Have you been involved?" that kind of thing. My Dad has passed away, but my Mom and sister kind of don't want to know.

MICKEY: How about fans approaching you? Do you feel uncomfortable about people approaching you and recognizing you?
WILL: I think it's very flattering, as long as they are respectful of my space. I'm not an ogre. I'm a really nice guy. I'm very approachable and I'd be very thankful that they took the time to say "hello" to me and tell me they enjoyed the movie.
MICKEY: How did you come up with Will Clark as the name?
WILL: I was actually given the name by Hot House. I did a film for them. It was the first thing I did. They came up with the name. I couldn't think of anything that wasn't cheesy. I was here in Los Angeles and I had two weeks to come up with the name. I still didn't have anything, and they said, "We already came up with the name because we had to put the video together and we had to come up with something real fast. We came up with 'Will Clark.' "
MICKEY: So you like it?
WILL: Yes, I do. At first I thought it was a little drab. But now I like it. Will was one of the names I had come up with, but I hadn't settled on a last name.
MICKEY: Well, thank you very much. And how does it feel to be

included in this book?

WILL: I'm very honored, it's quite exciting to be in your first interview book. You spotted me very early in my career, and I appreciate that. I think your recognition of my talent has really helped me quite a bit. Thank you. You've made it great.

The Bare Facts

Birthday: March 9, 1968
Zodiac Sign: Pisces
Chinese Zodiac: Monkey
Hair: Red
Eyes: Brown
Height: 5 feet, 8 inches
Weight: 165 pounds
Cock Size: 8 inches
Favorite Color: Sky blue
Born: Wausaw, Wisc.
Resides: New York, NY.
Workout Schedule: One hour a day, four times a week.

Videography

Are You Being Served?, *All Worlds Video*
Arousal, *Titan Media*
Big Mountain Retreat, *Titan Media*
Bound to Fool Around, *Projex Video/Close-Up*
Country Hustlers, *Oh Man! Studios*
Dr. Goodglove, *Hot House Video*
Federal Sexpress, *Minotaur*
Hard Core, *All Worlds Video*
Hell Bent for Leather, *Catalina Video*

Hot Firemen, *Centaur Films*
Hunk Hunt 15, *Stallion*
In and Out Express, *Minotaur Films*
Indulge 2, *Forum Studios*
Invaders From Uranus, *Thor Productions*
Island Guardian, *Titan Media*
Johnny Come Home, *Brush Creek*
Just Boys, *New Age Pictures*
Kink, *Stallion*
Leather Obsession 5: Mission Possible, *Forum Studios*
Liquid Latex, *Can Am*
Making the Team, *Man's Best*
Man Watch, *New Age Pictures*
Mission Possible: Leather Obsession 5, *Forum Studios*
New York After Hours, *Close-Up Productions*
Night Walk, *HIS Video Gold*
Private Parts, *Mustang/Falcon*
Stiff As Nails, *All Worlds Video*
Street Smarts, Sex Ed 5, *Minotaur*
Tail End Of Summer, *All WorldsVideo*
Take it Deep, *Man's Best*
Take One: Guys Like Us, *Hot House*

"Big"
Peter Dixon

"My feeling is that if you're going to be naked you might as well be as sleazy and nasty as you can be. It's nice to know that I'm in the fantasies of my fans. Knowing they're out there keeps me that much harder."

A talented multi-media artist, a creative, funny, writer and a huge, um, following is what makes Peter Dixon a pornstar worth including in any porn, er, appendage. Yeah, it doesn't matter what Peter Dixon does outside of porn, he's always going to be noted for his huge attribute, and his "Big" first name. (He hates that Catalina added "Big" to his name, but hey, it stuck.) And, by the way, if the shoe fits—and this is bigger than any shoe,—well …

Yes, he's bigger than his dick. And smarter and cuter. I first met Peter at Chi Chi LaRue's Birthday Party, the annual bash that brings all the bigwigs of the porn business together. Today, he is a columnist at *Gay Chicago* Magazine and a fellow reviewer of porn. Hopefully, his fans will get more from him than what "meats" the eye.

MICKEY: OK, you know I'm going to have to ask this one. How did you get your nickname "Big Peter?"

PETER: It sort of was to try to emphasize the size of my cock.

MICKEY: It does!

Photo courtesy: Jocks Studios

Photo courtesy: Catalina Video

(Left) **Big As They Come II**, (Above) **Men of Lake Me**

PETER: Uh, thanks.

MICKEY: Let's get right down to it. When did you realize you had an enormous cock?

PETER: I didn't know for a long time. Very early after I turned 18 I had a boyfriend who was bigger than me, so I never thought I was anything special.

MICKEY: That's incredible.

PETER: Yeah, Eric was pretty incredible, and then I started fooling around with guys in college and they thought I was huge, and that's when I realized that maybe I did have something a bit special.

MICKEY: Yeah, I'm sure that it was hard to find someone that filled Eric's, uh, shoes?

PETER: Well, I think there's only been three guys that I've been with who've been bigger than me.

MICKEY: How about anyone in the porn business?

PETER: Actually, there's no one in the business that I've been with, yet who's bigger than me. There are not that many, are there?

MICKEY: Well, my friend Jeff Stryker.

PETER: Ah yes, Stryker—I like him.

MICKEY: I also heard that you've worked with Jeff Stryker recently as a stripper in a show he did?

PETER: Jeff has always had a certain fascination for me. I have met a lot of people in the business. I've shot with Chi Chi, been pummeled by Joe Romero, hammered Kurt Stefano, talked tricks with Chuck Holmes, been shot by John Rutherford, gotten directing tips from Josh Eliot, been photographed by Rex Chandler, flip-flopped with Chip Daniels, gotten up close with Karen Dior and much more.

So, if truth be told, there was a little part of me that was curious if the sizzle in Stryker's eyes was a thing that translated to the flesh. As we shook hands there was no electric shock of body contact and I never even made it fully into the dressing room. I decided there was no point in pursuing the matter.

MICKEY: How do you feel about being in the adult industry?

PETER: For me the best part of taking part in pornography is the forum it provides to show alternative sexual lifestyles; the availability of this forum, I believe, leads to an more open and healthier sexuality for all. Not to mention it's a lot of fun.

MICKEY: How did you get discovered?

PETER: I was working in the Bijou Theater in Chicago dancing and an agent saw me there. I also worked a lot in Man's Country, the big bathhouse in Chicago.

MICKEY: Did you have fun dancing in the bathhouse?

PETER: You know, my feeling is that if you're going to be naked you might as well be as sleazy and nasty as you can be. I'd rather be naked and showing it in a bathhouse than in a bar with so many restrictions. It's kind of fun.

MICKEY: You sound like you're an exhibitionist?

PETER: That's the exhibitionist part of me. I like the sex with good looking guys, too. You shouldn't be ashamed of the human body, or sex.

MICKEY: Is there anyone you really enjoyed having sex with?

PETER: Dino Phillips was a great guy, he was my very first scene. They called me 15 minutes before and said "let's do it," and I didn't have time to think about it, really. I was a little nervous, but everyone was so nice on the set. I did an oral scene.

MICKEY: I heard you had good stories about getting horny with other dancers in the dressing rooms before the show?

PETER: There's all sorts of unseemly goings on in the dressing rooms. The highlights are high school locker antics complete with belching, farting, b.o., bull shitting, and single and group jack off sessions, or fluffing.

MICKEY: That's definitely a porn term—tell us all about it.

PETER: Fluffing can get down right randy. Those doing the fluffing might be co-workers, staff, customers. If it is a customer doing the fluffing your fellow dancer might actually be working. It's all well and good. But in the long run it's kind of like the mile high club. Fun for the novelty, but unless there will be no other opportunity there are better places which are a lot more fun and conducive.

MICKEY: Do you prefer to top or bottom on video?

PETER: I like to top. I like someone who is a sleazy bottom, someone who I can go to town with.

MICKEY: Any problems with someone who couldn't take you?

PETER: Well, once Marc Saber was so afraid that he had to be playing with himself with dildos before he was ready to stuff it up there.

MICKEY: Personally what do you like in your sex life outside of porn?

PETER: I like being a top, and a bottom sometimes, I'm versatile.

MICKEY: You have an interesting hobby—I hear that you're an accomplished artist?

PETER: I made a living off of the art for awhile, I'm a kind of mixed media artist who compiles a bunch of photo copies, paint, parts; I call it xerography. We did a show with a few other artists, put together a show called "Manhood," and over 700 people came to see it.

MICKEY: I'm sure it was a hit.

Photo courtesy: Centaur Films

From **Bustin' Loose**. Small wonder why Catalina tacked "Big" onto his name.

PETER: Tom of Finland's people heard about some of the artwork and wanted to see it. It takes up a lot of time.

MICKEY: Congratulations! What kind of guy are you attracted to?

PETER: I like someone with a dark look, some hair, and I also like the blond tanned look.

MICKEY: Do you have a specific kind of diet?

PETER: Sort of. In my diet I try to keep away from all fats, but I'm not always that successful.

MICKEY: How often do you work out?

PETER: I work out five times a week.

MICKEY: And have you had fans approach you since your video?

PETER: Yeah, I've been recognized. I just smile and say "thanks" to them for appreciating my work.

MICKEY: Have there been any fan problems?

PETER: Sometimes people get sleazy. That doesn't bother me, but it depends on the venue. If it's in the bathhouse it's one thing, if it's in a nice restaurant it's another. Sometimes you just have to be polite and pull their hands away and grind your crotch into them so they can't grab you.

MICKEY: What about the industry surprises you?

PETER: How everyone seems to work together. It's nice. The biggest complaint I have is that I'm not in Los Angeles. Everyone behind the scenes, the directors and all, are very friendly.

MICKEY: It was nice to meet you at Chi Chi's birthday party.

PETER: Everyone was so friendly there. I'm a bit shy in those situations, but people were constantly making an effort to talk to me. I had a blast there, though, it was a good party.

MICKEY: Anything you want to say to your fans?

PETER: It's nice to know that I'm in the fantasies of my fans. Knowing they're out there keeps me that much harder. If you note, I don't do more than four a year. I like to try different things. I don't necessarily care about being a star, more about being a player. I want to keep a good rapport with the industry and use my position to promote a healthier, balanced sexuality among gays. I will do any charity work for a good cause. My art work is still going; you can find more information about it on www.fota.com. Did I mention I also teach art to kids?

MICKEY: Are you dating now?

PETER: Dating can be a unnerving experience. Relationships can be absolutely cataclysmic.

MICKEY: Has it affected relationships in the past?

PETER: My starting to strip was one of several major factors leading to the break-up of my eight year, live-in relationship. Wow, eight years, I still can't believe it—you know that's 56 in fag years.

MICKEY: Truly! So how do you deal with that now?

PETER: If I met people I was interested in getting to know better I was really at a loss as to how to mention my dancing. Do I casually slip it into the conversation on a date? "Oh I hate the way my underwear wedges into my butt while watching movies, it's just like my g-string when stripping." (*Laughs*)

MICKEY: Did you ever date someone in the industry?

PETER: Yeah, I tried guys who were in similar professions. Dancers, escorts and porn actors. Yeah. You can see the problem right there. Find one without a sugar daddy, drug problem, self esteem issue, not needy— ooh there's a big one—not first and foremost materialistic—man, I'm still amazed at how many people that eliminates—*and* with the time to date. I batted zero.

MICKEY: And now?

PETER: For now I'm broadening my search base and I will date outside the city, even outside the state. I have been seeing a few guys, but all are a good 2,000 miles away. Oddly enough, dating someone long distance does have its advantages.

MICKEY: In what way?

PETER: It's easier for me to concentrate on the other aspects of my life and with the distance and time between visits it allows me to look at the relationship more objectively.

MICKEY: You're not giving up are you?

PETER: Not at all. My search for a man is not over.

The Bare Facts

Birthday: May 5, 1963
Zodiac Sign: Taurus
Chinese Zodiac: Rabbit
Hair: Blond
Eyes: Blue
Height: 6 foot, 3 inches
Weight: 178 pounds
Cock Size: 10 1/4 inches
Favorite Color: Aquamarine
Born: Chicago, Ill.
Resides: Chicago, Ill.
Workout Schedule: One hour a
day, five days a week.

Videography

Born to Be Wild *Catalina Video*
Bustin' Loose, *Centaur Films*
Down in the Dunes *Catalina Video*
Gypsy for Dicks, *Bijou Video*
In the Bushes, *Karen Dior*
    Productions/Video 10
The Men of Lake Michigan
    Catalina Video
Private Parts, *Mustang Video*
Room Service *Catalina Video*
Sleeping Booty, *Sex Video/Video 10*
Toilet Room Trilogies, *Bijou Video*

Photo courtesy: Peter Dixon

Eduardo

"When you hear Eduardo you are not thinking I'm a white West Hollywood boy, you are thinking I'm Latin. Eduardo—am proud of that. I love my name. That's my real name. That's me doing porn."

Swarthy, cocky and oozing with macho, Eduardo strode over and planted a big kiss on my cheek with a hot, sweaty hug. The hairs on his chest tickled me, and he had just ejaculated all over the bejeweled cape that co-star Marcello Reeves was wearing in **The Matador**. Director Michael Zen giggled as we greeted, and knew he had a winner of a video on his hands, raving about Eduardo's performance, both sexual and not.

We were at Chi Chi LaRue's famous rancho estate in West Hollywood, home to many parties and many more porn shoots. None of us knew at the time that this would be the last adult movie filmed there, because Chi Chi would soon move to the San Fernando Valley.

Anyway, the scene was being shot in the transformed bedroom of porn pup Jordan Young, and Eduardo slipped on some tight black trousers as he prepared for our interview.

Boyfriends for four years with fellow pornstar Sam Carson, this sexy Cuban man hadn't had sex with his lover on video until recently in the porn story about couple's abuse **Said and Done** (in which Matt Bradshaw plays the abused lover, and Sam and Eduardo are friends who watch helplessly). It took a while for his day in the sun to come, but Eduardo well deserves the recent honors—nominations for his role in **Matador**, at the *Adult Video News*, *Gay Video Guide* and Probe Men in Video awards. With his gravely voice, charming smirk and seductive eyes, he'll always remain one of the spiciest Latinos and among the hottest men in gay videos.

MICKEY: It's about time they found a good role for you. This **Matador** is probably the best role you've ever done, isn't it?

EDUARDO: Definitely.

MICKEY: Are you happy with your work?

EDUARDO: It's OK. Good. I was thinking this was a good role when

Eduardo

From **Sexual Suspect**

I heard about the project and then they found me and asked me to be a part of it. I don't know if they chose the right person.

MICKEY: Well, they did choose the right person. I just talked to director Michael Zen, and he said that when he saw you doing the role it was incredible. He was amazed how much you got into it.

EDUARDO: I think so. I did.

MICKEY: What do you think of the acting part of the porn business?

EDUARDO: No. I love it. That's what I wanted. That's why I wanted to do this movie in particular. I was doing just sex movies before and they were good, but this is the first time I'm doing a lot of acting.

MICKEY: And working with a master like Michael Zen?

EDUARDO: Michael is behind the camera and behind the scenes in everything, he is an expert filmmaker. I've seen that he is more worried about the acting than sex.

EDUARDO: So I like that I'm doing acting. That's my profession actually.

MICKEY: Really, you studied acting in college?

EDUARDO: I went to college for that in Cuba.

MICKEY: So you're from Cuba?

EDUARDO: Yeah.

MICKEY: And you studied acting there, like stage and film?

EDUARDO: Yeah. I mean really theater, some film.

MICKEY: And how was that in preparation for adult videos?

EDUARDO: Everything has helped me. Over there, I was an official actor. Then I went to Italy because my instructor was there. I lived there a few years and I get here to L.A. and am looking for work.

MICKEY: You couldn't get mainstream acting jobs, so you did porn?

EDUARDO: Well, yes. So here after a year I was starting doing my first porn, and then the other ones, but that's why I am really happy now about acting.

When they called me and Michael Zen told me you are going to be Jude, and you are going to be this and that. I was so excited. I told him that's what I really want. To me this movie is not like a porn movie.

MICKEY: So do you watch your movies? Do you ever see the finished product?

EDUARDO: No no. Not at all. Sometimes I can be someplace and I can see a video that I'm in. I think I should watch myself more often on camera, it would be a good idea.

MICKEY: Why is that?

EDUARDO: I think it's really good to watch yourself sometimes. Not for the sex part, I'm not thinking about sex when I'm watching it. I'm just watching because I want to know the way that I look. How my body can be changed, how can I look better for the next one, the way that I'm doing everything.

MICKEY: Does that make you uncomfortable, watching yourself?

EDUARDO: Sometimes I am so afraid of the way that I look and I just want to look better and do something better on the next one. It's like a profession you know. If you really care about this business you have to care about your work. It's not just a movie for money, pay your rent and that's it. Oh, no, it's a real profession.

MICKEY: Your boyfriend doesn't have a problem with you being in the business?

EDUARDO: No, because he is in the business.

MICKEY: That's good. Also, well, this is about bullfighting. Have you ever seen a bull fight live?

EDUARDO: Yeah.

MICKEY: You have?

EDUARDO: My father was involved with this business.

MICKEY: He was a matador?

EDUARDO: He's from Spain. It was in Spain and he got his training there, then he came to Cuba when he was 22 years old. He was doing that bullfighting when he was 18, I think. He's told me something about this before, when I was a kid, and I was watching movies, he told me about it. And my family is from Spain and Spain is crazy for it, how we say, it's really popular there. I mean this is like a tradition.

MICKEY: Bullfighting originated in Spain then?

EDUARDO: It's really from Spain. It's not from Mexico, no. It's from Spain. And my family originated from there.

MICKEY: Had you met Marcello Reeves before?

EDUARDO: On a set a few times and all that, but he had sex with somebody else and I had sex with somebody else.

MICKEY: Do you have sex with him in this one?

EDUARDO: He has to give me the opportunity to make him come, but I'm giving him a massage and that's it. There's no sex but we have to have this sexual tension. So we were talking about it and we are going to do something together this next year.

MICKEY: You started how long ago?

EDUARDO: In early 1995. In the last year I was thinking it's time to stop and just do good movies with people that are with good directors so that I know I'm going to be in a good movie.

MICKEY: So you turn down work?

EDUARDO: I have telephone calls from people and sometimes I

make some excuse and sometimes I say "no," but it's true, this is not about money. I want to be sometimes in a really good movie and I don't care how much they're going to pay me. I know that it's good and I'm going to be good and it's with good people. Sometimes it's true, of course, I may need the money because I have to pay bills, but that's why I don't do that any more, I am more careful.

MICKEY: Well, that's good.

EDUARDO: And that's why I called Michael Zen after he called me first because I didn't know him at all, but I did research and I heard he was a good director.

MICKEY: Had you ever thought about having a last name? Because you are one of the few male stars who don't. It seems like only the girls have one-name names—have you ever had any flak for just one name?

EDUARDO: No. You know what happened? I'm really proud that I'm Cuban. That I'm Latino. I don't want to be hiding my heritage; I can say I'm Latino.

MICKEY: But you could pass for white very easily.

EDUARDO: Exactly, that is the issue. My family from there are from Spain. I have green eyes. So I can say that, but I don't want to hide. I'm Latin. I just want to say my name just for that. When you hear Eduardo you are not thinking I'm a white West Hollywood boy, you are thinking I'm Latin.

MICKEY: Do we want to tell people that's your real name?

EDUARDO: It's no matter. Eduardo—I am proud of that. I love my name. I want to save my name and I'm also proud doing porn. So there is no way I can change my name. That's my real name. That's me doing porn. I don't want to have another name. No, that's me doing porn. The same person that you see right here.

They want to change my name in the movies, OK, I can be Michael. I can be Brian or whoever as the character, but my screen credit is always Eduardo.

MICKEY: Has any one ever asked you to shave your chest?

EDUARDO: Yeah.

MICKEY: You've never done that?

EDUARDO: No.

MICKEY: Good for you. Good for you.

EDUARDO: Well, before, yeah. Before, when I was starting, I was shaving. That was a big mistake because I'm a very hairy guy. And nobody liked me when I was starting. I was chubby. I didn't work out in my life. I mean if you rented a movie of me two years ago—oh, man, you would kill yourself.

MICKEY: I've seen them. I remember.

EDUARDO: Oh man. I was shaving my hair all over my chest.

MICKEY: That's funny, and the fans say they don't want people who shave their chests.

EDUARDO: That's right. And then after I let it grow everybody liked me. And after a year and a half everyone's calling me, calling me, calling me. All the time.

MICKEY: Yeah. Sometimes it just hits. Good for you.

EDUARDO: I'm working out now and I'm going to be going three months more and then I'm in ideal shape.

MICKEY: Can't wait!

The Bare Facts

Birthday: February 15, 1968
Zodiac Sign: Aquarius
Chinese Zodiac: Monkey
Hair: Brown
Eyes: Green
Height: 5-foot, 8-inches
Weight: 170 pounds
Cock Size: 8 1/2 inches
Favorite Color: Blue
Born: Havana, Cuba
Resides: Los Angeles, Calif.
Workout Schedule: One hour a day, four times a week.

Videography

Alex's Leather Dream,
  Close-Up Productions
All About Sex, *Thrust Studios*
Alley Boys, *Catalina Video*
Bewitching, *Bacchus Releasing*
Born To Please, *Video 10*
Brief Tales, *Blue Men/Sunshine*
Cheap Motel Sex,
  Bacchus Releasing
Chicago Erection Company,
  Catalina Videos
Clubhouse, *Totally Tight Video*
Customer Service,
  LeSalon/Brush Creek Media
Dallas Does Hawaii,
  DT Productions/Bacchus Releasing
Desert Train, *Titan Media*
Fault Line Sex Time,
  Close-Up Production
Fully Serviced, *Scorpion/Video 10*
Hair Trigger, *West Hollywood Video*
Hairway To Heaven, *Brute Films*
Hairy Chested Hunks,
  Close-Up Productions

Hard On Demand, *Video 10*
INNdulge Palm Springs,
  Catalina Video
Jeff Stryker Underground,
  HIS Video Gold
**Knight Men #3, Thick
  & Throbbing,** *Leisure Time*
Latin Obsession, *New Age Pictures*
Latin Showboyz, *Latino Fan Club*
Leather Bound,*Video 10*
Leather Men 1 & 2, *Video 10*
Leather Obsession 6,
  Forum Studios
Leather Triangle,*Video 10*
Leather Virgin,
  Leather Entertainment
Leather Weekend, *Video 10*
Long Play, *Triple X Productions*
Lost Loves, *Close-Up Productions*
Love Money, *Catalina Video*
Male Order Sex, *Metro Home Video*
Marine Fever,
  Brick House Entertainment
Matador, *All Worlds Video*
Men Together,
  Carl Stanyon Productions
Men With Tools 2: Nailed,
  Forum Studios
Mountain Jock, *Catalina Video*
Naked Truth, *Catalina Video*
Natural Born Driller,
  Big Bone/Video10
No Faking It,
  Scorpion Entertainment
Online Connections,
  Brush Creek Media
Physical Exam,
  Close-Up Productions
Portrait of Lust, *All Worlds Video*
Priority Male, *Catalina Video*
Pure Sex, *Bacchus Releasing*

Raw Discipline,
  Projex Video/Close-up Productions
Raw Street Meat,
  Midnight Man Video
Rip 'n' Strip Wrestling,
  Close-Up Productions
Said & Done, *All Worlds Video*
San Francisco Sex, *Video 10*
Sex and Sensuality, *Catalina Video*
Sex in Leather, *Video 10*
Sexual Suspect, *Catalina Video*
Shoot 'N' Porn,
  Pleasure Productions

Straight Men: Caught on Tape,
  Brickhouse Entertainment
Studio Tricks, *Catalina Video*
Sudden Urge, *Jet Set Productions*
Things You Can Do in Leather,
  Video 10
Threesome. *All Worlds Video*
Tools Of The Trade,
  Totally Tight Video
Try Again, *All Worlds Video*
Weekend Sex Camp,
  Close-Up Productions
Wet Warehouse 2, *Forum Studios*

Photo courtesy: All Worlds Video

On the set of **Matador**

Adam Hart

"I told my girlfriend I was coming out here to dance. And in a sense I am dancing, but I'm dancing on somebody's butt."

One of the hottest moments I've ever had in porn was being in a 110 degree hot tub, naked, with Adam Hart for this book. Naked in a small hot tub with this blond god—me! How lucky I thought I was. But, before you think that anything more extra-curricular happened, I was also with my sister (yes, my sister!), and Adam seemed a lot more interested in her than me.

What a flirt he is. I've known Adam since the first video he made, and went on the set in a bar for **Nights in Eden**, the Studio 2000 hit that put him on the map. I've also visited him at his house in Tampa, Fla. and befriended his girlfriend. Yes, this guy likes to suck cock, but he has a girlfriend, too. He's got a charming Southern drawl, which makes him endearing to men and women alike.

Fans love him. They gave him Best Jack-Off in the 1996 Probe's Men in Video Awards, and he was nominated for Stud You'd Most Like To Spread 'em For and Best Overall Pornstar but lost both to Ken Ryker. However, he hosted the event (wearing cute heart underpants), and the crowd loved him.

His work has often been nominated for awards, most recently as Best Actor for **Hard Core**, at the 1998 *Adult Video News* Awards. He's always jovial, friendly and welcoming with a big goofy bear hug and a grand smile.

The first part of this interview takes place at a noisy gay club in Orange County. The last half takes place quietly in front of my fireplace, and in the hot tub.

MICKEY: What was your favorite video role?

ADAM: I think one of my favorite was definitely the one where we first met, in **Nights in Eden**. That's the one where I'm playing a bar manager trying to get this cop from the straight world into the gay world and he's basically come out and I'm helping him. He comes over to my

Photo courtesy: Hart Productions

In **Hart Attack**

house and gets in the hot tub and that's where the sex happens.

MICKEY: And that cop is played by a longtime friend of yours, Joshua Sterling, right?

ADAM: Yeah, he used to work for me as a dancer—Josh used to do some hot work for me as a dancer. I have 16 guys dance for me at clubs all throughout Florida, gay and straight clubs. They all know what I've done in the porn video business, and they don't care.

MICKEY: Do any of them ask you about getting into the business, like Josh did?

ADAM: Sure, they sometimes ask me. I've been able to recruit a lot of the hot new guys into the business, such as Dean Glass, Tom Sawyer, Brian Heath. They are interested in it and they ask me about it, even though most of them have girlfriends. Believe me, there're going to be more coming.

The more I direct movies with my own production company, the more hot new guys I'll have, most of them from the dancers I hire. We dance mostly straight clubs throughout Florida.

MICKEY: How many of the guys you work with on the dancing circuit are gay?

ADAM: The percentage of my guys who are gay, let's see, they are half, about 50 percent are gay or bisexual, but I don't like to get into the personal life of the guys.

MICKEY: Now, with Joshua Sterling—it was one of the first times you ever had sex with someone who was a close friend of yours. You actually have to break in some of these guys, sometimes, right? Especially some of them with your own company, Hart Productions, I would imagine.

ADAM: With Joshua Sterling it was the first time I ever did a scene with one of my guys, and it was particularly difficult because it was his first time ever on film and he's fucking and everyone is watching him.

MICKEY: I can imagine that's kind of tough.

ADAM: Well, yeah, and he's like me because he's the kind of guy who likes to get to know someone before he jumps in the sack. In this business that's hard to do.

MICKEY: I guess it is!

ADAM: It's true, man—usually, in this business, you fly in from another town and it's like wham, bam and I'm out of here. Then, you go back home. That's how it is for me. That's what I was thrown into the very first time I did a scene.

MICKEY: It was as impersonal as that?

ADAM: That's what I did, I shook the guy's hand and the next thing you know he was bent over with his butt cheeks spread out in front of me. The first time for me on video was with Rick Bolton.

MICKEY: Did that go well?

ADAM: I guess it did, I enjoyed it, and he seemed to, he squirmed a lot, you know. You know that it works when you don't have to talk, you just go with the rhythm, and that's how it was. He has a nice butt—you remember him before he retired?

MICKEY: I sure do, the perfect bubble butt, and a real sweetheart.

ADAM: Yeah, (*smirks*) and with him it was a great way for me to enter the business. We got along together and our personalities are similar, but I just feel like it would have been better if I had the chance to meet the guy and get to know him first.

MICKEY: So did you handle that differently with your guys in your own production company?

ADAM: Of course. I pair up guys with guys who they are into, you know? It's something I've always wanted to do and I figure if I'm going to make videos, I'm going to do it right. I said I wouldn't perform anymore, but if a good role comes along like **Hard Core** did, with Chi Chi LaRue, I just couldn't turn that down. When I retired two years before, I thought that would be it.

MICKEY: After your first time on video, having sex in front of everyone, you decided to go with it and do more? There was no hesitation at all?

ADAM: It's no big deal once you've done it once. I like the attention and all, but it's no big deal. You're having sex in front of people, so? I don't want to make the big amount of videos that other guys do when they come into this business—that's the problem—I want to pace myself. Some guys do so many and they get all burnt out and I think that you can only expose your body to so many before the public gets bored with you. I'll do gay and bisexual films for a few years more and take a break again.

MICKEY: Doing your own videos gives you the chance to do some things that can improve the quality of videos. What is it that you have wanted to bring to the adult industry?

ADAM: As far as the way videos are made, I want there to be more of a one-on-one romp where the guys are truly into each other. I am bored with the same old situations where they play the weird music and do what is expected. I want to lead the public into thinking *this* is going to happen but then give the twist and do something totally different and let *that* happen.

I want to bring in some dialogue and some storylines, and I think I have in the first few videos that I've directed. Some guys out there like plot and story and some of my fans say that they don't.

MICKEY: Do you actually watch porn videos?

ADAM: I watch videos to learn. I used to watch three or four porn tapes a day and jack off to them and beat off three or four times a day, but now that I make them I don't watch them for excitement as much. I just can't get off on them like I did before.

MICKEY: Is there something you'd like to do on video that you haven't done before?

ADAM: I'd like to do a bisexual film that someone else shoots. I don't have anyone in mind, but she's got to be really pretty. Sharon Kane sounds like a nice person, I'd like to do a scene with her from what they all say about her. If I'm going to fuck a girl, she'd have to be real pretty like Sharon.

MICKEY: And does that mean you're bisexual?

ADAM: I don't like to classify myself. I've been with women, I like to be with men. I don't like the labels. The best I can say is that I'm just me, whoever that is. I'm just myself. I don't classify myself gay, bi or straight. I let the public decide who I am.

MICKEY: That means you're bisexual.

ADAM: Yeah, I guess so.

MICKEY: How have the fans treated you, since you've been in the business so long. You've been recognized for years—is that still a thrill?

ADAM: The fans have been great. A lot of them ask me if I'm gay, bi, straight. The way I see it is that I'd like the fans to decide. What I mean by that is let them have their fantasy and whatever you see on film, that's me. They've not seen me in everything I do in my personal life and they shouldn't.

MICKEY: Where did you grow up?

ADAM: I've been in Florida for six years; I'm from Iowa, that's where I grew up. I lived in Iowa for about 20 years. I lived on a farm. The Midwestern accent is kind of a Southern mix because of my Florida influence. But it's true, I was born and raised on a farm. I rented videos while I was living in Iowa and would sneak them around. I'd get in my Mom and Dad's stash. That's what I did to find out about sexuality.

While we were sitting at the bar in Orange County, a young fan named Reginald said that he has always admired Adam Hart and that he used to imagine that he would have a boyfriend just like him. Adam smiled and thanked the guy. Reginald asked for an autograph and Adam took his shirt off and took off his T-shirt underneath it and signed it to the young man, who clung to the white T-shirt with wide-eyed disbelief. He then ran over to his friends, squealing.

MICKEY: That was sweet of you.

Adam Hart

From **Hard Core**

ADAM: I like signing autographs. It makes me feel good that they appreciate what I do. It makes me feel good they notice me. I've not had any backlash from fans. A few critics here and there say something bad about me, and I listen to it and try to change it.

MICKEY: You've had a load of different looks—long hair, a ponytail, short hair, buffed and beefy—and when you started in 1992, you were a lot skinnier. What is your workout schedule now?

ADAM: I work out four days a week. Five years ago I started; I was a very skinny kid. I gained 28 to 30 pounds and I'm still growing. I'm not into that steroid junk—feel this, it's all natural. [*He makes a huge biceps muscle.*]

I've learned by watching other people and talking to trainers, that kind of thing, and that's how I learn. That's how I did it, I just started to train and eat good foods. I used to be really really thin. I'm still gaining like crazy. I'm six foot and 215 would be just right for me.

MICKEY: Is there something else that you'd rather do if you weren't making videos?

ADAM: I'd like to go into modeling more. Something other than just the adult entertainment industry. I'd like to get into International Male's magazine. I want to get into fashion modeling or something like that. I'm still new to this, relatively, so I don't know that much about modeling. I know I can pick it up easy.

MICKEY: What about learning a role and doing the acting that's required in porn videos more and more these days.

ADAM: I have no problem with the acting. I pick it up quickly, too. They design the scripts around me now, I've reached that level in the business, and it's real simple for me to say it all and learn the script right away. It's hard to get other people to say the lines, though. I know as a director it's tough to get it just right and get a performance out of people, you know.

MICKEY: What kind of guy do you like?

ADAM: My attractions? I like people who are shy. I'm dominant and I'm the aggressor. I'm a Leo. I like to be in charge to an extent. I like people who are shy, quiet, have good morals, good beliefs. I like farm girls, farm guys, you know, country girls. Someone who isn't real outspoken. Even if you do find somebody who's shy, it's not easy to find someone who can deal with what you do. You're a sex addict no matter which way you look at, you know what I mean? I've dated a couple of girls, a couple of guys, and they just can't deal with it.

MICKEY: Does porn have an affect on your personal relationships?

ADAM: At first they say, "Oh, oh yeah, I understand," but then they try to change you. When it comes down to it, it's hard. They try to get me out of the business and that's not right; this is what I like. People want to mold you. They come home and watch your videos but they don't want you to be a pornstar.

MICKEY: Does anyone in your family know what you do?

ADAM: My family doesn't know anything about it. They know I'm interested in producing adult film and directing it but they don't know what I've done already. They're not really judgmental. I keep my business end separate from them. It's better off that way. I'm the only one in the family, not a spoiled rotten one, neither.

MICKEY: Is there anyone in the adult business who you'd like to work with? A guy as a partner?

ADAM: I'd like to work with [Jeff] Stryker. Neither one of us have ever bottomed and I think it would be good for the public to see. I said to him I'd put 10 grand down into the project if you let me be the one. He has a great ass, and as far as I'm concerned he's still the tops in the business.

MICKEY: You've met Jeff Stryker? That must have been quite a moment.

ADAM: He's a legend for nearly a decade and still has it totally together. He's on top. I'd like him, mmm. I like him. The reason I like Jeff so much is that he's taken some time out to tell me about the business. I don't want to be like him, I'm very happy with myself, I have my own self. He's told me what to expect, what to do, what not to do. He's like a big brother type figure. He's from the Midwest and I'm from the Midwest; we're cut from the same cloth, I guess.

MICKEY: You've worked with John Travis, the man who helped discover Stryker, and did some of your best work with this award-winning Hall of Fame director.

ADAM: I think John Travis is great. He's had hits like **Powertool** and **Score 10** under his belt, and I'm honored he put me on the box of **Hart Throb**.

MICKEY: That was the one that turned a lot of heads in the video stores, with you and the sunburned opened crotch pose prominently displayed.

ADAM: I enjoyed that video. I liked the dance scenes in the strip clubs, particularly, and liked when I was doing nude push-ups.

MICKEY: Adam Hart has sort of become an institution these days, hasn't he?

ADAM: Studio 2000 opened the door and marketed Adam Hart and people wanted to form a partnership. I have another job outside the

Photo courtesy: Hart Productions

Adam Hart recently hanging around his house

business, too, and it's not that easy. But it's been good for me.

MICKEY: Anyone give you some great words of wisdom for others who may want to make it into the business, or think they can do porn?

ADAM: I remember Jeff Stryker told me when I first got in the industry, "When you're seeing the money you're making in this, you're going to want to form your own company" and I said, "Never," and here I am with my own company. It's hard once you get into that type of lifestyle and make the connections and meet people who want to represent your work—well, it gets personal and you get close friendships, like me and you.

MICKEY: Thank you.

ADAM: But I think I would tell people to find a good agent. They're out there. Yeah, because I really don't want to deal with the nitty-gritty. It gets tough when you're dealing with production companies and different directors, and I feel an agent can get you better money.

MICKEY: So it's been helpful for you.

ADAM: Yeah, but when it comes time to give up that commission you wonder if you really needed him! I do miss David Forest very much, and I'm sorry he's in jail.

MICKEY: What do you do when you're not always interested in the person you're with in a sex scene.

ADAM: That's a good question. It's the most frustrating part of the business. And that's why my girlfriend and I made this commitment on New Year's that I wouldn't do it anymore, and actually I told her that all I was doing on this trip was coming out here to dance. And in a sense I am dancing, but I'm dancing on somebody's butt.

What I do sometimes, what I have to do, is fantasize about her.

MICKEY: What is the biggest misunderstanding about you?

ADAM: People ask me, "How can you be straight and still get hard and stick your dick in some guy's butt or like sucking a dick?" Well, maybe I'm just a little bit this side of being heterosexual. I'm somewhere in that middle part. I feel like some of the other models have slapped the gay community in the face with saying they're straight and all that and I don't think that's right. I know I'm not completely straight.

MICKEY: There's a rumor that you've got your new lover involved in this last project of yours.

ADAM: My secret lover, yeah.

MICKEY: So it's true?

ADAM: Well, put it this way: it's someone I've known for a long time.

MICKEY: Hey, wait a minute—I've also heard rumblings that this could be your brother working in your next video.

ADAM: Who'd you hear that from?

MICKEY: Can't tell.

ADAM: You've got good sources.

MICKEY: So this is really your swan song in porn? I've heard this from you before, and you've changed your mind before.

ADAM: In front of the camera it is. I'll always be involved in some way. I love it. I love the business and the people in it.

MICKEY: What's going on with your new plans for the business?

ADAM: I have a new partner and we're wanting to do something in the Matt Sterling quality of videos. I am going to put out about five movies a year, but they'll probably be with people you won't forget, and ones you may not know. We'll have high budgets, hot new models and realistic fantasies.

MICKEY: Are there any aspirations for mainstream movies?

ADAM: I've had people say to me, "Why aren't you doing legit films, why are you doing this? How can you do this? Why aren't you doing something real? Why aren't you making a real living?" There are some people who are quick to criticize.

MICKEY: So what do you tell them?

ADAM: My answer is that I am doing what I want to do, and they're just jealous because they can't do what they want to do.

MICKEY: And that's what?

ADAM: Well, they can't fuck handsome men and get paid for it.

The Bare Facts

Birthday: August 7, 1969
Zodiac Sign: Leo
Chinese Zodiac: Cock
Hair: Blond
Eyes: Baby blue
Height: 6-foot
Weight: 198 pounds
Cock Size: 8 1/4 inches
Favorite Color: Yellow
Born: Iowa
Resides: Tampa, Fla.
Workout Schedule: Two hours, four times a week.

Videography

Deep Desire,
   Hart Productions (director)
Fame & Flesh, *HIS Video Gold*
Hard Core, *All Worlds Video*
Hart Attack, *Hart Productions*
Hart Throb, *Studio 2000*
Just One Favor, *Forum Studios*
Nights in Eden, *Studio 2000*
Sexologist,
   Hart Productions (director)
Tainted Love, *Catalina Video*
Takedown, *Studio 2000*
Voyeur, *Studio 2000*

In **Hart Attack**

Sonny Markham

"It may be a strange way to come out, but porn helped me. I love the fact that there may be thousands of fans out there who beat off to me on video. I think that's cool."

When Sonny Markham decided to come out, he did so in a big way. The buffed, rippling-muscled go-go dancer on the Chicago nightclub circuit was engaged to be married to a girl he knew since high school. He knew that men liked to watch his bubble butt wiggle, but he never understood that. He had plenty of gay friends, but he never really was attracted to them—well, not back then anyway.

Suddenly, while dancing nude at one of the country's longest-running gay bathhouses, Man's Country, in Chicago, Markham took the dive and gave gay sex a try. He came up wanting more. Club owner Chuck Renslow immediately contacted his friend, noted gay director John Travis, of Studio 2000, and told him about Markham's sudden turnaround, and how he might now do porn movies.

Travis—who helped groom the careers of superstars Ryan Idol and Jeff Stryker—knew about Markham and had wanted him nude in front of a camera lens for years, but Sonny always resisted, claiming he was heterosexual.

"I saw immediate star quality in Sonny, and I think he has superstar potential," Travis sums up. "Audiences love him."

So, Travis not only put Sonny in Sonny's first porn video, but his co-hort in porn Scott Masters, wrote a script of Markham's true-life coming out story—sexual encounters and all—and decided to film it at the actual spot where Markham's deflowering occurred, the bathhouse. The video, **In Man's Country**, remains a big hit in video stores.

In his first-ever interview, Markham shyly says he's happy to return to where his new life began, at the club in Chicago, to tell us how it all

Photo courtesy: Studio 2000

From **In Man's Country**, the famous Chicago bathhouse where some of *this* interview was conducted.

happened. He just performed a stylish strip in a gangster-like zoot suit in front of more than 1,000 guys who braved the storms of the Midwest—some fans even flew out from Washington, Florida and New York—in order to see Sonny in person.

Markham always took care of his body, which is why he danced for the Meatpacker's dance troupe in Chicago. He danced for women, but there are few clubs catering to that, so he danced also at gay clubs where the tips and money were better. He often rebuffed the advances of the men at the club who became his fans.

Director Travis hosted a lively question-and-answer session, with the men in towels after the video screening. People asked him what it was like shooting in the bathhouse, and what he saw in Markham as a star.

"Sonny has this innocence and boyish charm about him that I knew immediately would be something that our audiences would respond to," Travis said.

Sonny also sat with me two years in a row at the *Adult Video News* Awards in Las Vegas, looking dapper and dashing in a tuxedo. He is as friendly as he comes across on video. And, he's always nice enough to drop by whenever he's in town on the West Coast.

MICKEY: Did you watch porno before you got into it?

SONNY: When I first got into it, I watched videos with Jeff Stryker and Ryan Idol, and I was really impressed by them. Sometimes I look at the magazines, but a lot of the magazines, they're hard to look at and say I do that or I'm going to do that. It's a little bit weird. When I step into the video I'm a different guy.

MICKEY: Do you watch your own videos?

SONNY: I don't watch my own videos if I can help it, I don't like to.

MICKEY: Do you still get nervous going to a shoot?

SONNY: I get nervous each time I do something, like the first time I met co-stars like Trent Reed, Scott Randsome, Chad Donovan, J.T. Sloan, Mark Montana—all those guys who are big stars I get nervous around. When we're together in a video I think: "this is going to be a great movie." But being with the big names is really scary.

MICKEY: Is there anyone in the business, past or present, you know you would like to work with?

SONNY: Yes, Scott Baldwin; yes, who else? Hmm, definitely Scotty, he's hot, he moved to New York. I have wanted to work with him since the time I met him. I'd like to work with Cody Foster; he's bigger than me. Tom Katt would be cool to work with, I like him a lot.

MICKEY: Is there a fantasy or situation you would like to do in video or real life that you haven't done?

Playing cowboy in **Mavericks**

SONNY: One situation is doing a guy and a girl where the girl is thinking "these guys are going to do me," and the guys mess around with each other more and it surprises them all.

MICKEY: Would you do a bi movie?

SONNY: I'd love to do that. I would hope that my fans would not mind if I did it. That would be great. Scott Baldwin wants to do that too, and that would be great to do it with him and a hot girl.

MICKEY: As far as a fantasy situation, you've done Westerns and some costume stories, is there any other genre that you would find fun?

SONNY: Well, let's see, maybe something like a hardcore leather scene. I've never experienced leather or been into that. If someone would chain me or do things to me, that might be great.

MICKEY: So you haven't gone downstairs in the Eagle here in this very building?

SONNY: No. When I first started here, I saw a guy tied to the wall getting whipped and I thought "Oh my god," and I thought, "Oh, no, not me." Maybe I'd do something like that if it was faked.

MICKEY: Guys came on to you a long time before you gave in?

SONNY: I never tried to be rude because, in a way, I was always curious. A year ago I started looking at pictures in men's magazines and wanted to be in the magazines with those handsome guys. Now I am and it's kind of strange for me. This is where I actually got introduced to things. Here is where I made some major changes in my life, I guess.

MICKEY: Once you passed those portals you never returned again?

SONNY: I know I enjoy sex. I love sex. I like when people appreciate my body. And that's kind of the ultimate thing, for someone to see you having sex.

MICKEY: Where do you see your porn career taking you?

SONNY: There's only one Jeff Stryker, and Ryan Idol is big, too, but if I can get up to a Tom Katt or Marco Rossi-level, that would be my ultimate goal so that I can go on the road and dance and make money. If I'm in it another year or two years I can get to that level.

MICKEY: Anything you want to say to your fans?

SONNY: I want to meet my fans, if people are actual fans of mine. If you see me and recognize me don't be afraid to come up and say hi. I'll respond, I promise.

MICKEY: You've come such a long way since we first met a few years ago. You've had great acting jobs, you've performed in theaters in the play **Making Porn** about the adult industry, and I loved you in **Dark Side of the Moon.**

SONNY: I had a great deal of fun with that one. Now that I'm in it, I

want to be the best I can. These guys saw me before, always saying "no" and always fooling myself. Now, I say "yes" and I'm a much happier guy.
(Sonny is drumming his fingers on the bar and his forehead is sweating.)

MICKEY: You don't have to be nervous around me!

SONNY: I'm really nervous about meeting all these people, people who you know in magazines, and people like you. I saw you in that documentary movie **Shooting Porn**. Then there's other guys like Jake Andrews, Ty Fox—I'm fans of you all.

MICKEY: Have you ever been interviewed before?

SONNY: No, I never have. This is my very first time.

MICKEY: I always like to break in the virgins.

SONNY: I'm honored to be part of your first interview book. I thought, maybe I'll be famous enough one day that Mickey Skee will interview me.

MICKEY: Oh, that's an honor. That's sweet, thank you. I don't know if you've realized how people are reacting. Have you had a sense of how you're hitting the industry?

SONNY: Its really kind of crazy. I look at those guys in magazines and they are so attractive that I always dreamed that someday I would be in their category.

MICKEY: It seems like you like kissing a lot. You've even kissed a few of the fans here.

SONNY: Kissing is the best. I enjoy the fans that I can kiss; I can kiss a guy, I can kiss a girl. I do really enjoy kissing a man.

MICKEY: Your tastes run the gamut, I know.

SONNY: I love transsexuals, drag queens, men, women. When I'm turned on, I do what I want to do, that's my philosophy, I don't know what that makes me. I'm not ashamed the next morning saying, "Oh my god, what did I do with that drag queen?"

MICKEY: Is getting more involved in the gay world helping you keep in shape, care about your body?

SONNY: Getting into the gay world made me comfortable with myself. I work hard on my body and people seeing it appreciate me, but I used to be ashamed of it and wear sweatshirts, sometimes two, to try to look bigger. Before, I worked out like a crazy man, eight hours a day sometimes. Then, as soon as I stopped going that much, I really had fun, when I let myself go.

MICKEY: That's a great change for you.

SONNY: The last two years of my life I've really had fun. More than anything else, the adult industry and the people in it have made me more comfortable realizing who I am. I love sucking dick, I love drag queens,

I'm sexual and having the best time of my life. It may be a strange way to come out, but porn helped me. I love the fact that there may be thousands of fans out there who beat off to me on video. I think that's cool.

MICKEY: Does your family know what you do?

SONNY: No. My family knows I model, but they don't know what I do. I have six older brothers; I'm the seventh son. I don't know if any of them fooled around with guys—I don't think so because they're very straight laced, but if it's in my blood, it may be in their blood.

MICKEY: So what made you decide that you wanted to do this?

SONNY: To get into the porno business? I've danced, and some people have said I should do porno. Then I got an opportunity to meet some of the porno stars when they came through Chicago. People say I'm kind of shy, but I am kind of show-offy about my body. I like when people appreciate my body.

MICKEY: You've decided to go with the Studio 2000 team exclusively from the outset?

SONNY: Right.

MICKEY: What made you decide that?

SONNY: After doing **Mavericks**, the first movie, I felt like I couldn't do this for anyone else. I was blown over from the exposure that I got, and the way it was on their sets, and so I got comfortable with them.

It was easy talking to everyone and dealing with them. In this business you have to depend on a lot of people. I still don't know anything about porno, so I have to trust somebody. I trust the people at Studio 2000.

MICKEY: My experience in interviewing guys is that there is one of three reasons, or a combination of them, that they usually give for getting into porn. They are either exhibitionists, they are doing it for the money, or they do it because they get to have sex with really good looking guys. Which do you feel are some of your main reasons?

SONNY: From the choice of those three, obviously I'm doing it for money. If someone said "you don't get paid anymore," I would be out of the porn business. I like the idea about the money.

MICKEY: What about being an exhibitionist?

SONNY: Yeah, about the exhibitionism, that's true for me, too, I guess. I like when people recognize me. I enjoy it when I'm in a different city and people say, "I loved your movie." I love that! When people say, "I've seen your pictures in this magazine or that and I beat off to them."

MICKEY: Have you had any bad experiences with fans?

SONNY: Bad experiences? Sometimes when I'm with somebody in a gay bar and people are pulling on you and trying to dance with you. I say, "How are you doing? Excuse me." I'm used to being grabbed at, I don't mind that, but when people just start pulling on you and won't leave you alone, that's enough. I've had it and I tell them so.

MICKEY: Do you get the sense that some people think that the people in this industry are all dumb guys who are good-looking?

SONNY: Sometimes. More than that, people—not all the time but a bunch of times—have said, "Let me suck your dick in the bathroom" and when I say "no" they're like, "Why not? You're in porno." I'm in porno, so do I want to do this all the time? I think not.

MICKEY: How do you deal with that? What do you say?

SONNY: I say "Not this time," or I will say something like, "You know what, it would turn me on if you would suck this guy's dick." I guess I have a real selective eye for guys. I know what I like.

MICKEY: Do you have a specific type?

SONNY: Yes, I have a specific type of guy. To hang around and be close to someone, it doesn't really matter what you look like, of course. But what attracts me is people with bodies like—oh, let me think of an example—like Christian Fox: a little shorter than me, hard body, but not as muscular as I am. That drives me nuts.

MICKEY: And blond?

SONNY: No, hair color is not important. But I like hairless. That kind of thing I like.

MICKEY: When did you first notice or find out that you had a big dick?

SONNY: If my dick is bigger than average, then—

MICKEY: Well, it is! Maybe not in the porn industry, but to the general audience it is!

SONNY: You know, I had never seen a lot of guys naked. But when you start to be in the dancing business and you start being with guys and stuff then you see a lot of guys naked. So then you get an idea of where you stand. I know I'm bigger than average because I've seen probably a hundred guys naked and I know I'm bigger than average from that. Because otherwise you look at magazines, and everybody has a 10-inch dick, and mine's like 9 inches or 8 inches, depending on how hard it is, and I feel like even with that I don't measure up.

MICKEY: What was your experience on the set of your first video, **Mavericks**? Did you have preconceived ideas about what the business was going to be like?

SONNY: To be honest with you, a lot of it *is* kind of how I thought it would be, believe it or not. In my first movie **Mavericks** I did the scene with Chad Conners and he was kind of like my type. I picked him out specifically. I like that. When we got to the set, it was an outdoor set on a truck, I looked at him and said "Oh, my god, he's beautiful." When all the lights were on and all the people were standing there I said, "Gee, it's a real movie" and I thought to myself, "This looks like a porno set." It's just what I thought it would be.

Other than that, though, the guys I got to meet and work with—a lot of them are really nice guys who are in college, and not like high school dropouts or runaways. They're not like that. And also the people who own Studio 2000—we're kind of like a little family. I didn't expect that. I expected it to be a little sleazier than it was.

MICKEY: So Chad Conners was the first person you did a movie with on video? And he is one of those guys who would consider himself "gay for pay" right?

SONNY: Yeah.

MICKEY: So were there any difficulties there?

SONNY: I thought that would be easier, and that's what I would desire is someone who says, "Hey, I'm just here to do my job." And really, it was great and he's beautiful and I felt that he was straight.

But I almost think now I would rather be with someone who tells me, "I love to get fucked." Like when I did the scene with Adam Rom in **In Man's Country**, he wanted me to keep fucking him after the camera stopped so he could have his cum shot.

MICKEY: Hey, what a concept—you like fucking gay guys?

SONNY: Yeah, I fucked him off-camera to make him cum. I could get into that because he was loving it. Now I'm thinking it's better to have someone who really likes it.

The Bare Facts

Birthday: July 27, 1976
Zodiac Sign: Leo
Chinese Zodiac: Dragon
Hair: Brown
Eyes: Green
Height: 5-foot, 8-inches
Weight: 192 pounds
Cock Size: 8 1/2 inches
Favorite Color: Purple
Born: Chicago, Ill.
Resides: Chicago, Ill.
Workout Schedule: One hour, three or four times a week.

Videography

Dark Side of the Moon,
  Studio 2000
In Man's Country, *Studio 2000*
Mavericks, *Studio 2000*
Trying it On for Size, *Studio 2000*
Working It Out, *Studio 2000*

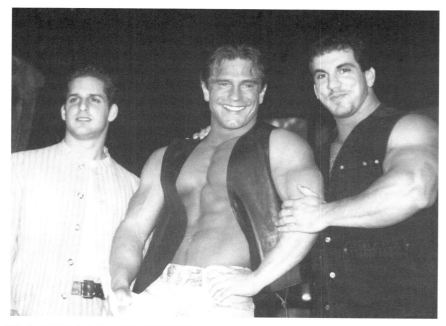

With Scott Baldwin (left) and Tom Katt (right)

Jason Miller

"I liked to get naked. I hate clothes. If I am at home I am usually in boxers, or if there's no one around I'll be naked, but it's a little bit indecent running around flopping out, you know."

H e doesn't look like your average pornstar, but he's the newest one of this bunch in this book, and he's reflective of the new generation of stars. The first time I met Jason Miller was with the old Jaguar Studios team, which was famous for making storyline movies back in the 1970s, like **Ghost of A Chance, The Experiment** and **The Roustabouts**. They became porn classics and brought gay adult movies out of the looped sex and into mainstream types of film. Jason has the same boy-next-door qualities, except this boy has piercings and long green sparkly fingernails and a shock of blond white dyed hair.

He's still as genuine as can be—no steroids, not even a workout plan. He made it as a star before he was 21. Yes, it's legal to shoot someone over the age of 18 having sex, but he can't have a beer until he's 21.

He smokes like a fiend, and loves stuff about aliens. I spent an evening hanging out with Miller and Czech stud Johan Paulik, who was in L.A. one night. We went to a gay bar in West Hollywood, where they got mobbed, and then to the Chateau Marmont bar, where the movie stars hang out, and then to Jerry's Deli for onion rings. These two guys represent the new generation of porn: fresh faced, natural, fun-loving and sexy.

Changing his name from Jeremy Lee to Jason Miller was a tough decision, but he wants to put some of his earlier videos behind him. He had bad experiences with them, and that's because he was a naive kid from Walla Walla, Washington. Director Kevin Clarke took his story and made a video about it, called **Pleasure Principle**, which, on Jaguar Studios' first try in almost two decades, is a big hit. It garnered a slew of nominations at both the *Gay Video Guide* Awards and the *Adult Video News* Awards (where Jason Miller was nominated for Best Screenplay).

Jason Miller

Photo courtesy: Jaguar Productions

The willy from Walla Walla in **Pleasure Principle**

The story, about a small-town gay kid looking for love, is Jason Miller's story. And, as director Clarke says, "You can't make this shit up."

MICKEY: So tell me how you got your porn name. Because "Jason Miller" is very boy-next-door. Is that the purpose of it?

JASON: How I got my porn name. Jason really was the name I really liked and they kind of made up Miller for me 'cause we were trying to think of a last name. We were going for a regular guy kind of name.

JASON: I think that's kind of why they picked that. Because we were going through names and I was saying that I liked "Jason" and then they said "how about Kevin?" "No, no not Kevin." "What about Brian?" "No, no," They were going through all these names and I was like Jesus.

MICKEY: No no, not Jesus! (*Laughs*) Did you want it to be sort of like your real name?

JASON: Yeah. It's very close to my real name.

MICKEY: So are you going to tell us your birth name?

JASON: OK, it's Jeremy.

MICKEY: You don't like Jeremy?

JASON: I hate that name.

MICKEY: Why?

JASON: I don't know. I just always hated that name. Ever since I was a little kid I hated that name. I always wished I had a different name and Jason and Nathaniel are my two favorite names and so it was either going to be Nathaniel or Jason for my stage name.

MICKEY: I like Nathaniel, too.

JASON: Nathaniel is my favorite.

MICKEY: You could've been Jason Nathaniel.

JASON: I thought about that.

MICKEY: So why get involved in porn?

JASON: When I was younger, I saw a porn film. My stepfather was watching it while I was in the kitchen eating. I kind of peeked around the corner, I looked and I was, like, "wow."

MICKEY: A straight porn film?

JASON: It was straight porn. It was a lesbian thing, too. It was obvious these two cow girls were really into each other and this guy comes along—that's when I got interested. It was great: he throws her down on the hay and starts going at her and I was going, "Wow!" I'm seven years old and my jaw is on the floor and since then I have been really interested in it.

MICKEY: Sex preoccupied you?

JASON: I've always been interested in sex. I don't know why. I didn't have sex until I was 18, but that didn't mean that I didn't think about it or want any. I was just really shy. So I didn't go after it. So since I was really young, I used to fool around with the neighbor boy.

MICKEY: Fool around?

JASON: Like, we just like played with each other. Little kid stuff. We'd touch each other's things.

MICKEY: What age was that?

JASON: I moved there when I was six or seven and I was about 15 when I moved out. I was in my mid-teens.

MICKEY: So after you saw those porn movies, you were hooked?

JASON: Yeah. I watched a few of them with him, too. They were straight ones. He would always get hard and then he'd always have to pull it out and show me how hard it was and ask me to touch it.

MICKEY: So you were comfortable with yourself and your sexuality at an early age?

JASON: No. I denied it. I told myself, "no, you're a boy. You are supposed to like girls." So I had this whole following of girlfriends. I had a lot of them, and they were always the most pretty ones. I found the most pretty girls and went after them and I always got them.

MICKEY: Wow.

JASON: But then whenever the subject of sex would come up or we would get too close, I'd back off and say, "I'm sorry, we are having our problems" and I'd run off before we'd have sex. So I completely used all those girls to cover up the fact that I was gay.

MICKEY: So obviously you knew you were not attracted to girls, but you waited 'til you were 18 to actually have sex with a guy—why?

JASON: A lot of guys would flirt with me and stuff but I was too shy to do anything back. So they kind of gave up—you know, lost interest. You want to know about the first time ,don't you?

MICKEY: Yeah. Of course.

JASON: OK. There was this guy named Peter. I thought he was really cute. I had just recently met him at one of my friend's birthday parties and I found out that he was bi and that he kinda liked me. So he was over at our house one day. Peter came over with our other friends, Maureen and Ron and Seth, so there was, like, five people total.

Ron left because Peter started rubbing his foot on my crotch, which was turning me on. Then Peter kind of went from there to stroking this girl, 'cause he's bi. I didn't know what I was, but me and this girl started going at him and we were taking turns with him while Seth was watching the whole time.

MICKEY: Sounds like a good beginning for a pornstar!

JASON: This is what told me that I knew I'd like to do porn, it's because it's the first time that I ever had sex, and I had somebody sitting there watching the entire time. It took four hours to do this.

MICKEY: Four hours?

JASON: Four hours and Peter finally came but it took him awhile. It was his first time, too. The fact that Seth was sitting there, watching, really turned me on, really big time. I kind of liked the idea of being watched.

MICKEY: So Seth was just sitting back and watching. He wasn't participating at all?

` **JASON:** No, because Peter didn't want him to. They were friends and he just didn't really like the idea of having sex with him but he didn't mind him watching.

MICKEY: Did you consider yourself an exhibitionist?

JASON: Yeah. I liked to get naked. I hate clothes. If I am at home I am usually in boxers, or if there's no one around I'll be naked, but it's a little bit indecent running around flopping out, you know. When I sleep, I sleep either in boxers or naked.

MICKEY: How did you transition into adult video?

JASON: I was living in Chino Hills. I had just recently moved down to California and I was sitting and chatting on the Internet one night and I saw this picture of Peter Wilde. He did one video for Junior Studios, it was one of those solo videos where they just beat off.

MICKEY: OK, that was **Boys Will Be Boys**.

JASON: Right. So I figured I would contact Junior Studios to see if— just maybe, possibly—I had a chance. I figured I would send them a picture. I sent Kevin Clarke one—it was the only nude picture that I had. I snapped the picture and then I scanned it on the computer and started tweaking with it and made weird, artsy-looking pictures out of it.

MICKEY: That's on your Web page, right?

JASON: That's right, my "killboy" page. So all you see is my torso down to my penis and it doesn't even have the balls so it's like the hard penis coming out up to my shoulders and that's all you see. And I sent him a face shot that was really blurry along with that and he sent me back the funniest e-mail. He was like, you know, "You seem all right and you've got a penis but you seem to have some kind of weird skin disorder. It's, like, because of the color. It was fuchsia and my skin looked plastic and shiny. It just looked really fake but it was funny. So we agreed a couple days after that that I would just go over to L.A. and I'd meet with him and here I am now.

MICKEY: Were you surprised how quickly you got a response?

JASON: Hell, yeah. Within a week I was living in West Hollywood and having all kinds of stuff happen that I didn't think would ever happen. Like meeting [Bel Ami exclusive Czech Republic model] Johan Paulik.

I spent an entire day with him and now I consider him a friend. He's not just somebody who is just pretty. He's the coolest guy I think I have ever met. So I was, like, "Wow, I had a lot of fun with him."

MICKEY: Did you get to fool around with him?

JASON: No. A lot of flirting, but no. The closest that we ever came to that was when he was peeking over my shoulder when I was taking a piss in a bathroom.

MICKEY: So once again you get to meet somebody who you've kind of admired from afar.

JASON: Yeah. I never thought that would happen. Even you, or anybody whom I've heard and read about. Look what I am doing right now, being interviewed for a book of pornstars, by famous porn reviewer Mickey Skee. Wow. If you would've told me a year ago while I was still in Washington that in a year I would be here doing this I would have laughed in your face and said you're high on crack.

MICKEY: Well, yeah. Hanging out with Johan, that was a pretty cool event. That was nice going out with him the other night.

JASON: Hell, yeah, that was.

MICKEY: How did the idea of actually writing your story in **Pleasure Principle** come about?

JASON: That was really weird. I didn't know that was happening. Kevin [Clarke, the director] started doing it and he was basing it on me. He kept asking lots of questions about my life and I never really understood why he was asking all these things. I don't keep secrets, so I figured I'd tell him. And then I see pretty much everything I told him on paper.

He made up some—a lot of it was fictitious, but it's stuff that I myself, if put in that situation, would've done. A lot of the things were true. The Walla Walla part was all real. I was born and raised there.

MICKEY: So tell me about it—you go back to your hometown with this movie crew and shoot an adult video? Did people there know you were going to do porn?

JASON: A few. I'd told a few of my friends that I was coming back to do that. I told my mother. My mother, yes: I tell my mom everything. I have a journal on my homepage on the Internet and I put up an e-mail that I sent to my mom. I got a lot of response back from that, saying, "You didn't send that to her, did you?" or "I don't believe you, blah blah blah."

People don't believe it; my mom is like my bud. She's like the coolest person on the planet. She had me when she was 18. So basically when she was growing up, I was growing up, and I had a lot of fun with her and she's always been my bud and I tell her everything.

MICKEY: That's incredible.

JASON: She was the first person in the family to know that I was gay.

MICKEY: But, did she know all along? Moms always seem to know.

JASON: She said that my step-dad had suspected it and told her and stuff and she was like "Oh, no no no" and kind of denying it and stuff but then, see, when I told her—the part in **Pleasure Principle** when she cried in the movie?—she actually did. She cried really hard. I went up to Washington and told her. It was one night; I wasn't living at home anymore. It was my feeling that it was right, and I told her right after I did the thing with Peter athat I actually knew that I really was gay because I actually had sex with a guy and I liked it.

MICKEY: How did she react to finding out that you were in porn? She couldn't have been very happy about it.

JASON: She's mostly worried that I'm going to pick up some kind of a disease. I caught hepatitis during one of my early shoots, I'm guessing it was during a video. I had no idea what hepatitis was. I had yellow skin. My eyes turned yellow. I got just horribly sick to where I couldn't get out of bed at all. It would hurt. I'd puke every five minutes. I couldn't eat anything and I found out that it was hepatitis when I finally went into the clinic. Luckily it was A-strain and it went away. It went away like the flu. But now I'm told if I catch it again it could kill me. I caught it bad. That almost got me out of porn. I had a couple of other bad experiences during some filming, too. Which I'd rather not talk about.

MICKEY: Yeah. I've heard.

JASON: Yeah. So I was just about over that hepatitis thing and that was it. I was going to completely quit porn. I went to the [second annual] Probe Awards and I was like, "I really don't need to be here." So I went to leave and I saw Kevin and we started talking and he convinced me to do this one video.

He was like, "This is what you wanted to do when you got into porn," which is true. This is exactly what I wanted to do when I started doing porn. I wanted to do one of the lovey, mushy-type, happy-little-perky-type films and I wasn't doing that. I was doing some dirty-slut-type ones where I was a leather top, which I'm not. I'm not a top at all. I can't top. I am definitely a bottom and they had me doing the dominating.

MICKEY: What was that movie?

JASON: That was **Blade Studs**. I didn't really feel comfortable with that one, trying to be all rough in leather. Drew Andrews and Peter Anderson are in that one.

MICKEY: Right. And that's for All Worlds?

JASON: Yeah. And **Reform School Confidential** is the first one I ever did.

MICKEY: Also for All Worlds. And how did that go?

JASON: That went fine. I was a little nervous at first. But once I start, I go off in my own little world in my head and I don't see cameramen; I don't, like, really notice directors. They'll tell me something and I'll end up doing it but I don't hear it, I kind of transpose it to where it's like a thought that I'm having that I want to do this now. So I visualize that they're not there.

MICKEY: You are very young in your career—have you ever been with guys who you haven't really particularly liked, they're not your type and you've had to train yourself to get it up for them?

JASON: Everybody who I was with was not my type, except, let's see, Brian Dickenson in **Pleasure Principle**, because he has been my friend for five years. I'd fooled around with him one time before but we never really went all the way.

MICKEY: Until you did it on video?

JASON: Right. And that was one of my best scenes. So he and James Sterling are probably the only ones whom I did a scene with whom I would've actually done something with on my own.

MICKEY: Who is the other one?

JASON: James Sterling.

MICKEY: James Sterling is a newcomer?

JASON: No, he's been in five or six videos, I think. He's not real well known but he's been in a few. He was in **Blade Studs**. I had to do the top on him. I was the leather top. We had been friends for about a week before that, not knowing we were going to do a scene together. So he knew what kind of person I was. So when I'm saying stuff like, "Suck that dick, boy," we would just bust out laughing. We laughed so much on that set. We laughed the moment I put all that leather on cause I'm head to toe in leather, which is not me. The whole thing was just—

MICKEY: Hysterical. That's hysterical.

JASON: I thought it was funny. I am curious to see how they got that to come out to. 'Cause if they got something good out of that I want to give them a congratulations because it's got to look totally goofy.

MICKEY: So going back to going into Walla Walla. Obviously there were a lot of people who knew you—it's a small town, right?

JASON: There is probably about 1,600 people there.

MICKEY: There are high schools bigger than that in L.A.

JASON: Right.

MICKEY: And you were walking around with a film crew? People obviously knew who you were. Were they asking, "Who are these guys and why are they filming you?"

JASON: Yeah. I was telling them that I was modeling and stuff like that. I wasn't telling them that it was for a porno shoot.

MICKEY: Kevin was worried at first that people would find out and they would get run out of town, but it was never that way?

JASON: No. No. No. It was not like that at all.

MICKEY: Nobody ever harassed you?

JASON: Not until after they were gone. Then I told most people, "By the way, remember when I was up here last? I was shooting a porno."

MICKEY: How did people react to that?

JASON: They were like, "No way, really? Here in Walla Walla?" They thought it was a trip. If you watch the video you will see there is Melody Muffler, which is a big thing in Walla Walla because they have these figures that they make out of muffler parts and car parts and stuff.

MICKEY: Right.

JASON: That's, like, a big thing in Walla Walla. That's why they filmed that there and then the grain growers, which is the big grain mill. There are very distinctive things that are definitely the town: my grandmother's video store is two businesses up from Melody Muffler. We were going to throw that in there and then we decided not to, because I would've been walking right by the store and my aunt was working at the time and she would've seen me walking by the store with these people filming me. I'd have to explain that one to her and decided, well, no.

MICKEY: Your grandma must have some adult tapes?

JASON: She does. She's got a room, a separate room for pornos.

MICKEY: Maybe they'll be stocking **Pleasure Principle** some day.

JASON: I don't know.

MICKEY: How was doing the outdoor sex?

JASON: The bugs were a bitch.

MICKEY: I've always heard about bugs. Yeah.

JASON: There was a ton of flies out there. That's why in the film I say "there's too many bugs, let's go back to the hotel."

And the whole time when I was blowing my partner, there's this little pine tree right behind me and it was tickling my ass the whole time and it was so annoying. There was no way to get around that because I was in the clearest spot that we could find there.

MICKEY: Were you happy seeing the results?

JASON: Yeah. I was. I was kinda shocked. I was, like, "wow."

MICKEY: Are you one of the guys who could get off watching

yourself on videos?

JASON: No.

MICKEY: That's kind of odd to you?

JASON: No. This is the first video that I ever watched that I was in. The previous ones, I haven't seen them. I have no idea what they are like. The first time I ever saw myself having sex was on some clips for All Worlds when they had this party for their new films that were coming out and I was in three of them. So they had me on there and I was going, "So that's what my ass looks like with a dick up it?"

MICKEY: Yeah. You never get to see that.

JASON: Right.

MICKEY: That wasn't frightening to you, then?

JASON: No, it doesn't bother me at all. I had my best friend of seven years sitting right beside me watching the clips, saying the same thing. "Wow, so that's what your ass looks like with a dick up it?"

MICKEY: Do you prefer to do bottom on camera?

JASON: Yeah.

MICKEY: Is that how you are in real life, too?

JASON: Until I started porno, I had never done it before. I was dead set against it. I wasn't going to do it and I was told that if I wanted this part—I needed money really bad at the time—I had to bottom and so I said, "all right, fine." But I had some bad experience with that and I didn't think I'd bottom again 'til I did the one where I got hepatitis but I actually liked it then because it wasn't as bad.

MICKEY: So it isn't what you would normally be doing?

JASON: Now it is. Hell, yeah.

MICKEY: So butt fucking is OK?

JASON: Yeah. I realized I actually do like it. I came harder with my ex boyfriend than I ever had before when he was fucking me.

MICKEY: What do you want to bring to the adult industry? Do you want to continue doing these kind of romance videos. Do you think that's something you'd like to see more of personally?

JASON: Yeah.

MICKEY: Like relationship-type videos?

JASON: Yeah. Yeah. What gets me is when two guys kiss. That turns me on more than anything. If I'm on the Internet, I'll see pictures of guys and stuff. I see, like, a guy giving a guy a blow job or something like that. I'm just like "Oh, yeah," you know. And then I'll see two guys kissing and I'll stop and I'll be like, "Oh wow, I like that."

MICKEY: And you know what? The audiences say that, too. The readers whom I get letters from all say they want more kissing.

JASON: That's good, yeah.

MICKEY: Because it used to be gay guys didn't kiss.

JASON: Yeah.

MICKEY: Because they thought it was faggy. It was supposed to be feminine if the guys kissed.

JASON: Whatever.

MICKEY: Luckily, because of the younger generation coming into it, like you, they want to see that. They want to see relationships. They don't want to see a straight guy, right? That's all of the stories have been way back, conquering the straight guy.

JASON: Right. Which is really degrading in a way, because it's presenting a bad image of homosexuality. Like we all want to recruit them and bring them in and turn them all gay.

MICKEY: Exactly.

JASON: I respect everyone's sexuality. Most of my friends are straight. They're all straight guys from Washington and they're all cool about it because they respect me. I respect them. I mean, of course, quite a few of them are very, very attractive and I'd definitely want to do something with them, but I don't, because I respect them.

Photo courtesy: Jaguar Productions

With Richie Fine (left) in **Pleasure Principle**

The Bare Facts

Birthday: March 18, 1977
Zodiac Sign: Pisces
Chinese Zodiac: Snake
Hair: Dark blond, white blond (today)
Eyes: Blue
Height: 5-foot, 11-inches
Weight: 140 pounds
Cock Size: 7 inches
Favorite Color: Purple
Born: Walla Walla, Wash.
Resides: Hollywood, Calif.
Workout Schedule: Not at all

Videography

Pleasure Principle, *Jaguar Studios*

Others under the name of Jeremy Lee

Blade Studs, *All Worlds Video*
Lambda, Lambda, Lamda,
    Hollywood Sales
Reform School Confidential,
    All Worlds Video

Steve
O'Donnell

"I prefer to dance totally in the nude—I think you're freer and you're not hiding. There's no tease when you're dancing up there with everything out."

I t's a small wonder that Steve O'Donnell does magic as a hobby. He makes magic every time he takes his clothes off on video. He can look every bit the part of an Aryan young god with his sparking blue eyes and short shock of yellow hair. Or, he can turn into a sweet, goofy kid; or a leather dominator; or the dreamy boy-next-door.

I first laid eyes on him at a club in Las Vegas. He was sweet, shy and eager to meet the famous drag directrixes (I had four of them around me) who were leaders of the porn biz. We talked, we had a few drinks, we even danced, and then I introduced him into the porn business and to some of the directors he would be working with in years to come. Then, I found out that not only did he know who they were (he had done his homework), but he had already shot a few videos that were ready to come out and take the industry by storm.

I'm not one to tell people if they're going to make it or not in the porn business, and mostly I think they won't, but this guy, I knew, had what it takes. He's not just another dumb blond, he's the ultimate blond. He's the most versatile performer on camera these days, giving a wriggling bottom performance or a hard-ramming top-performance depending on what the script calls for, and what the director wants. Every director he's worked with has raved about him, his dick and his personality. The fans rave too, especially when they meet him in person, and he won Best Newcomer his first year out, picked by the fans at the Probe Men in Video Awards.

And, after being introduced to famed director Jerry Douglas, he inspired a script out of Jerry that will incorporate Steve's magic (and Nazi Germany and gay men). It's a chilling and brilliant idea, and although I'm sworn to secrecy, I can guarantee: it will be magic!

Photo courtesy: Montana

Steve O'Donnell poses in his latex gear.

MICKEY: Has Jerry talked to you about working on the new project he's writing just for you?

STEVE: Yes, I'm very excited about working more than just in a cameo on a Jerry Douglas movie. You can tell he is a great director, but hey, aren't we supposed to keep this a secret?

MICKEY: Yeah, I know, OK! How did you get your name?

STEVE: Well, people say I look like Chris O'Donnell, and I wanted to keep my real first name, so it seemed like a natural.

MICKEY: And how did you get started in this business?

STEVE: To make a long story short, I met a roommate of a friend of the agent Peter Scott, and Peter Scott is now my agent. He got me connected to porn videos.

MICKEY: Did you know about videos?

STEVE: I love porn videos; I used to work in a video store in Michigan.

MICKEY: Did you have a favorite porn star?

STEVE: Matt Gunther. He has a great body.

MICKEY: Did you get to meet him before he died?

STEVE: Yes. Four years ago I first saw him live and saw what a great chest and great nipples he had. The whole package of his body was great; he's the kind of guy who would be my fantasy guy. My favorite pornstar, without question—even before I knew about the politics or people in the industry, or anything else—is definitely Matt Gunther.

MICKEY: Then you saw him after he got sick with AIDS, right?

STEVE: Yeah, I knew he didn't blame the porn industry, he blamed his drug habits and his own personal sexual irresponsibility. I read an article about it, it may have been yours. Then, I saw him at the Probe Men in Video awards, the first one, and he was in a wheelchair and you made the presentation with him and I went up and talked to him afterward.

MICKEY: That's right, I heard about that, he tried to pick you up! Even from a wheelchair, he was always a big flirt. Unfortunately, he didn't make it until the next year's Probe awards.

STEVE: Yeah, that's a shame.

MICKEY: What incorrect ideas or wrong perceptions did you have about the industry that have changed since you shot a few videos?

STEVE: From a shooting standpoint, the viewpoint of the lights and cameras are all pretty much what I expected; but from the outside, people think it's a bunch of dirty old men behind the camera—that's not the case at all.

MICKEY: Are you interested in the camerawork?

STEVE: I'm always asking questions about how things are done on the set; yes, I'm very curious about it.

MICKEY: And have you had any bad experiences yet?

STEVE: Everyone's been a kick. I enjoy being on the set a whole lot.

MICKEY: Nothing bad at all?

STEVE: No, not really. I think the wrong perceptions started in the early 1980s when there were a lot of drugs everywhere, but I haven't seen any drugs whatsoever on the sets.

MICKEY: That's right: everyone still thinks it's like it was shown in **Boogie Nights**. It's nothing like that.

STEVE: No, the drugs are not like what you see in the movies, and never on the sets.

MICKEY: Anything that you heard about that you found out is reality in the adult industry?

STEVE: I heard about the fluffers, and there are fluffers, and that's a sexy job.

MICKEY: For those of you who don't know, a fluffer is someone who helps a star get hard and stay hard but never appears on camera.

STEVE: And some of them are quite cute and have incredible cocks.

MICKEY: So I've heard.

STEVE: And they give some nice head.

MICKEY: Anything you would say to someone who wants to get into the business?

STEVE: Do it without regrets. Do it and don't be afraid.

MICKEY: You aren't sorry you've stepped into this world?

STEVE: I have no regrets getting into it; I enjoy it.

MICKEY: How do you think you look on video?

STEVE: I haven't seen myself on video very much. A few have still got to come out that I'm looking forward to seeing. I hate to hear myself, I hate to hear my own voice, that's why I don't do karaoke.

MICKEY: You go on dance tours too, don't you?

STEVE: Yes, I've danced at La Cage and I've danced in Washington, D.C.

MICKEY: You get to go fully nude in Washington, so I hear—is that true?

STEVE: Yeah, I prefer to dance totally in the nude—I think you're freer and you're not hiding. There's no tease when you're dancing up there with everything out. I like dancing on top of the bar.

MICKEY: They loved you in Washington, D.C., so I hear?

STEVE: D.C. always welcomed me, they were great. Sure, there was an occasional grope or someone got drunk, but it never got unpleasant. I hope to go back and dance there.

Photo courtesy: Oh Man! Studios

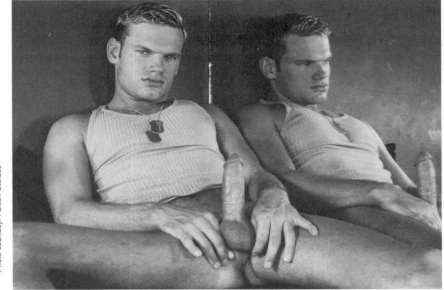

Photo courtesy: Falcon Stuidos

(Top) In **Flavor of Men**, (Bottom) in **Stripped**.

MICKEY: Maybe now that you're an up-and-coming pornstar and have a Probie under your belt you can ask for more money.

STEVE: I like my Probie, I like the ones that look like giant dicks. Those are great. I'm sorry that you guys changed the award to make it look more respectable.

MICKEY: You're right, I'm sorry they did that too. I'm not sure that porn awards should look like anything but a big dick. Anyway, I'm sure you'll win others before your career is over.

STEVE: Thank you!

MICKEY: Could you have a relationship with someone in the business?

STEVE: It takes a lot of self esteem to have a relationship with a guy in the business if you're from outside the business and don't understand it. I had a boyfriend for a year-and-a-half and we broke up when I got into the business, and I miss him, but I'm not sure he would approve of how involved in the profession I've gotten. He certainly wouldn't like the position I'm in now, where I get recognized and that sort of stuff.

MICKEY: But you have a nice boyfriend now, and that's been going on a while, and he seems cool and isn't part of the business, right?

STEVE: Yeah, he's a good guy, and we love each other very much. He comes with me to awards shows, especially the ones in Vegas.

MICKEY: Now let's talk about some kinky things.

STEVE: Sure.

MICKEY: You seem to like these latex gloves, and I was on a photo shoot where you posed with them.

STEVE: Yeah, I do, it's like having on five condoms at the same time.

MICKEY: You like rubber better than say, leather.

STEVE: Yeah, since I'm a vegetarian, liking leather would be a bit hypocritical.

MICKEY: What can we see you in soon? You always have something coming up.

STEVE: This year there're some I'm working on for Catalina, Studio 2000, BIG Video, and then the Men of Odyssey project sometime in the future.

MICKEY: Are you still doing magic shows?

STEVE: Sure, I'm doing magic any chance I get, working on new routines.

MICKEY: Where are you from?

STEVE: I'm from Michigan, it seems like a lot of pornstars come from there for some reason.

MICKEY: That's true, I guess they grow 'em bigger there and they keep better.

STEVE: Yeah.

MICKEY: What is your favorite music group?

STEVE: 9 Inch Nails

MICKEY: You say that you are a vegetarian—why is that?

STEVE: I think about what I eat all the time and how I'm affecting the environment. I did a lot of learning about how they're cutting down rain forests for breeding cattle, and that was the last straw for me. I do have to watch what I eat.

MICKEY: You have a truly boy-next-door air about you.

STEVE: I'm not one of the gods, I'm just one of the guys.

MICKEY: Do you aspire to be one of the big names in porn?

STEVE: I'm just an average guy; if the career takes off, then it does.

MICKEY: Have you ever worked with a straight guy?

STEVE: I worked with Chad Knight in a Studio 2000 video; it was a bedroom scene. He was much quieter and much shorter than I expected.

MICKEY: Do you have any trouble with the guys who come into the business and aren't gay-identified like you are?

STEVE: I have no problems with straight guys being in the business, even if it does seem to be a bit ridiculous. If he kisses beautifully and gives the best blow jobs, what difference does it make?

MICKEY: Where do you see yourself as far as the adult entertainment business?

STEVE: Being a pornstar for some people is ugly and common, but I hope to be one of the memorable ones, like Joey Stefano, Chad Knight or Ryan Idol. For me, getting even close to that status would be great, rather than every other Joe Blow. But, if I don't that's OK, too.

In **Raw Material**

The Bare Facts

Birthday: May 20, 1969
Zodiac Sign: Taurus
Chinese Zodiac: Cock
Hair: Dirty blond
Eyes: Metallic blue
Height: 6 feet 1/2 inch
Weight: 155 pounds
Cock Size: 8 1/4 inches
Favorite Color: Metallic, industrial colors
Born: Michigan
Resides: Las Vegas, Nev.
Workout Schedule: Whenever I get to the gym.

Videography

Alley Boys, *Catalina Video*
Cat Men Do, *Catalina Video*
Code of Conduct 1: Stripped, *Falcon Studios*
Download, *Falcon Studios*
Family Values, *Men of Odyssey*
Flavor of Men, *Oh Man!Studio*
Flesh and Blood, *All Worlds Video*
Grease Guns 2, *Studio 2000*
Heatwave, *Falcon Studios*
Hot Cops 3, *Centaur Films*
Indulge, *Forum Studios*
INNdulge Palm Springs, *Catalina Video*
Law of Desire, *Catalina Video*
Lucky Strokes, *Fox Studios*
Malibu Beach Hunks, *BIG Video*
Party of One, *Catalina Video*
Raw Material, *Hot House*
Sex and Sensuality, *Catalina Video*
Sexual Suspect, *Catalina Video*
Street Smarts, Sex Ed 5, *Minotaur*
Striptease, *All Worlds Video*
Ultimate Reality, *Minotaur*
Vacation Spot, *Forum Studios*
Working it Out, *Studio 2000*

Jeff Palmer

"Before a scene I stop sex for at least two weeks. I get so horny I am going to explode. I get to the set and say, "Where's the kulo, where's the hole?" and I want to go in there and rip somebody apart. I just want to go in there and fuck like a horse."

He had just come out from a two-hour, sweaty workout, flashing his bright smile and emerald green eyes. Jeff Palmer hopped in my red convertible and I caught a faint whiff of clean sweat and expensive cologne. As soon as he got to my house, he plopped on the sofa with his legs spread, rubbing his bare arms, bulging out of his tight yellow tank top. His camouflage pants and boots seemed uncharacteristic of his squeaky clean image, as did his many rings on his fingers. But, that's all part of the image Falcon created for him.

But the Jeff Palmer sitting in front of me still has the stunning eyes, the bushy eyebrows, the thick, gargly accent and the cockring wrapped around his wrist. He still talks about enjoying and having wild sex, and growing his sideburns.

This is the first interview that he's ever granted anyone, and alas, he says it could be his last. He's tired, and retiring from porn for now, but someday we may all get his foreskin back again.

MICKEY: You haven't given out any interviews before, have you?

JEFF: This is my first interview ever, John [Rutherford, director of Falcon Studios] is very protective of me.

MICKEY: Yes, it took a while to convince John to let me have you all to myself here, but he trusts me. I'm glad to do your first interview. And, we're planning to put you on the cover of the book.

JEFF: That is very exciting to me.

MICKEY: OK, how did you land in this business?

JEFF: I got discovered in Miami. There was a guy there who takes some photos of stars and he asked to take pictures of me. He took some bad pictures, some Polaroids, and sent them out to people.

Jeff Palmer

In **Stripped**

MICKEY: Then they got them at Falcon?

JEFF: Yes, they saw them and wanted to meet me. I have always been with Falcon. I still have a contract with them. I am not sure if I will finish it because I'm not sure I want to do videos anymore.

MICKEY: You don't want to do videos anymore? But you're one of the hot new stars, you're on top!

JEFF: I have three more scenes to do for them in my contract, but I'm not very much interested in it anymore. I decided I didn't want to do it. I'm sometimes bored.

MICKEY: Don't disappoint the fans now that you just got started. You are not saying "never again" then, so I'm hearing?

JEFF: I learned that you can never say "never" and I don't say that I will stop forever. If I say that, then it may change. I just keep on going and when the situation changes again or if I feel like doing it again I will do it. You see, it's important to me that when I'm not 100 percent sure then I will not feel good about doing it; and I'm not going to do it well if I don't feel into it.

MICKEY: Why are you stopping now?

JEFF: I don't know—because I don't feel like I'm doing quality work. You have to have quality in whatever you do. And even if other people say [my work] is good, I don't believe it right now.

MICKEY: You've been nominated for a slew of *Adult Video News* awards and you won the prestigious Best Erotic Scene at the Gay Video Guide Awards for **Manhandlers**.

JEFF: Yes, that was all very great. It was a very exciting show.

MICKEY: I know a couple of the guys in this book have taken some time off from the business and have done very well making a comeback after a short sabbatical. You can do that too, and I don't think you will find that that will hurt you.

JEFF: I may take a year off, I may not come back.

MICKEY: Either way, you will be missed. You just came back from your workout today. Do you like working out?

JEFF: I work on my abs a lot. Someone told me about working on my abs. I work on one muscle a day, plus abs always: I do biceps and then abs, then triceps and then abs.

MICKEY: And why always the abs?

JEFF: I had no abs at all, and one guy told me I had none and he traumatized me. So now I work on that: not the ass, the abs.

MICKEY: What did the people say when you went to Falcon?

JEFF: They said, "Oh you look so much better than in those pictures we saw about you," and they took new pictures of me. Before I did my

Jeff Palmer

first movie they asked me if I would feel comfortable and I told them I was very comfortable with wild sex. That's what I like—wild sex.

MICKEY: I'm sure they are very happy with that.

JEFF: They all were really happy with that. It gets tiring, though; I see that everywhere. I was going to do something for the spiritual side of me, at the MMC Church, and there was someone there who recognized me as Jeff Palmer and said "What are you doing here?"

MICKEY: Are you very spiritual?

JEFF: I think I am. I was raised as an evangelist, with a very strict religious background.

MICKEY: And you not only are spiritual, you have a new dildo coming out later in 1998. How did that work?

JEFF: (Laughs) You have to get your dick hard. You put it then in this long tube of liquid, it's white gummy stuff. You have to keep it in there until the stuff gets hard. I get hard and have a cockring on so that I stay erect and I breathe and wait a few minutes and you see the space of dick and veins and all that.

MICKEY: Everything will be just like your own cock?

JEFF: Everything will be just like me, exactly the same. I don't know if they will do the foreskin or not, they haven't told me yet.

MICKEY: Why did you initially go into porn?

JEFF: I needed money really quickly.

MICKEY: But you obviously care about what you do, too?

JEFF: You can have quality in whatever you do. All your feeling has to go into something, only then it means that you're giving 100 percent. I believe in that. It has to be in your heart, then you have quality. So, if you have doubts, don't do it.

MICKEY: And that is why you have stopped the business for now?

JEFF: Yes, that is why.

MICKEY: Do you watch your own videos?

JEFF: I don't watch my own videos.

MICKEY: Never?

JEFF: Well, sometimes I do; but most of the time, no. I don't want to hold on to the past. There's no day like today. Looking into the past can make you not very happy. Not always, of course, but sometimes.

MICKEY: What has been your favorite video?

JEFF: I did have a lot of fun with **Manhandlers**. I was pretty much into it, and it was what was real sex for me. I don't want to include other people that I haven't checked in with, but there was a relationship that I was ending for that video and it was my way of ending it.

MICKEY: You looked like you were having a great time and you were playing to the camera.

JEFF: I was feeling so good that I was having fun. I spent two or three weeks without sex, so that when I was on the set I was so excited that I was going to explode.

MICKEY: Is that your secret? You don't have sex for two weeks before a shoot?

JEFF: That's right. Before a scene I stop sex for at least two weeks. I get so horny I am going to explode. I get to the set and say, "Where's the kulo, where's the hole?" and I want to go in there and rip somebody apart. I just want to go in there and fuck like a horse, like I'm raping someone.

MICKEY: So, that makes you really horny to wait so long.

JEFF: Oh yes, it makes me so horny to stop having sex. I just want to fuck like a horse and fuck a hole. I don't care if the person likes it or not, just don't get in my way.

MICKEY: Tell me about working with John Rutherford.

JEFF: I would not be Jeff Palmer if it weren't for John Rutherford, all the credit goes to him.

MICKEY: Did John come up with that name for you?

JEFF: No, no, no. John didn't come up with Jeff Palmer; it was this guy who was fired from Falcon, or something. Maybe that's what the reason he was fired for, probably, was giving me that name. I didn't like the name. I thought of Frabricio, and when I met John he kept calling me Paco. I don't like Jeff Palmer … But it sticks.

MICKEY: What is your ethnic background?

JEFF: I'm from a little town in Argentina. I have some family from Italy, and part from Spain.

MICKEY: You're not from Buenos Aires? Everyone from Argentina seems to come from B.A?

JEFF: No, I come all the way from this little town, it's very small. I liked Argentina because it's a little bit of everything: hot, cold, jungle, desert, snow and everything. It's fun and the only thing is the difference in culture.

MICKEY: Meaning?

JEFF: Well, for example, I didn't realize it until later, but there are no black people there. Not even one. When I went to Brazil and when I saw a black person I stopped to stare because I was shocked. That makes the culture very racist. I didn't know the culture was so racist.

MICKEY: It's also very Catholic, right?

JEFF: Now it is becoming very much Protestant and everybody is trying to get you and say "this is the way." Catholics say "this is the way;"

Jeff Palmer

In **Stripped**

Protestants, Jewish, Buddha, all say "this is the way." I would think "how the hell are you going to find the right thing," and I realized that in *all* the ways it is how you talk to your conscience which matters.

The only thing you have to do is pay attention to your conscience. It's when you follow that that you dream of God and God talks to you, not in books. He's talking through something much better and that is you conscience.

MICKEY: That includes your sexuality, too, right?

JEFF: Yes.

MICKEY: I know you went to visit director and former pornstar Kristen Bjorn down in Miami recently—how was that?

JEFF: Kristen Bjorn was very great, and he talked a lot in Miami about these things. He said, "I don't believe in god but I believe in karma, and he taught me to remember that sex is not bad, it's good.

MICKEY: How did that affect you?

JEFF: Some other people, they're saying things like, "You shouldn't have sex, you should make love and not just have sex." I decide to wait to hear what my conscience is telling me.

A card falls mysteriously, without wind, from the mantle of my fireplace.

JEFF: See, that's God talking. (*We both laugh*)

MICKEY: It's heavy stuff.

JEFF: I am still finding things out.

MICKEY: Do you consider yourself bisexual, straight, gay?

JEFF: Bisexual, if it means I can choose to have sex with a woman or a man. It is so I am able to have sex with a woman and a man, but it's easier with guys because they are able to treat you in a good way and satisfy you with all the areas. Women just satisfy you only in sex, not emotional, you have to satisfy her in those ways. It's so hard to find a woman to satisfy in all the areas you want.

MICKEY: Don't people accuse you of being straight?

JEFF: Yes, people say because I'm happy being a top that I'm straight, and that's not true, that's what they think. People say it would be better for me to say I am straight because fans would like me more, but I will not lie to you. I am not straight.

MICKEY: The gay community doesn't like to hear that you're bisexual, either.

JEFF: Yes, that's true. People don't like to hear about it . They get hurt because those are the people who want to be satisfied and don't want me to be able to satisfy anybody else. Guys can satisfy a guy and if he also can satisfy a woman, the gay guys don't like it at all, the males get jealous of that. They say it's a threat and they cannot compete with it. Not true.

MICKEY: Have fans every been inappropriate to you?

JEFF: They want you to be nasty and sometimes I would want to be nasty with some of them, sometimes I'm not. Fans and people come up to me all the time.

MICKEY: How do you handle it when a fan comes up to you?

JEFF: Sometimes, I say, "Oh yeah. Everyone says I look like him." I don't say it's me. Sometimes you like being recognized, sometimes you don't like it, but if they ask, "Are you Jeff Palmer?" and I like the look of that guy, I may want to meet that guy. If I feel like it, yeah. That is when I will be Jeff Palmer.

MICKEY: That means you may fool around with a fan?

JEFF: I have had people say and do inappropriate things to me and many expect me to be nasty like I am in the videos, but I will tell you a secret: I only am that way when I want to be nasty, that's when I become Jeff Palmer. I am him when I want to be Jeff Palmer, and when I say "Yes, I am Jeff Palmer" then I want to be him with you.

My neighbor, Sharon Kane, who lives downstairs, then comes up to bring up a load of laundry. She just dyed her hair red and he says he likes it that way. Jeff Palmer knows Sharon well and calls her "Mama." They talk about her pet pig, Candy. Then, we get back to interviews.

MICKEY: Physically, what do you like in a guy?

JEFF: Sexually, for sex, I like someone physically attractive, so I don't like a 60-year-old man or something like that. I like somebody who is a pig, really like a pig.

MICKEY: Not like Sharon Kane's pet pig?

JEFF: Oh, yeah, maybe that, too—I'd like them to squeal like a pig. Somebody who is really into sex, squealing, that's what I like in sex.

MICKEY: Do you have any preference? Taller, blond, hairy?

JEFF: No, anybody. Whoever is a pig.

MICKEY: OK, is there someone out there you would like to have sex with in the adult industry?

JEFF: I don't watch too much porn. Sometimes they tell me I can pick who I like but I don't see that much and I just say put me with whoever is a pig that's all. I don't know many guys who are a pig, a real sex pig. I've written a script for that.

MICKEY: What? You wrote a porn script?

JEFF: Yes, something that John Rutherford may do someday. I can't tell you about it, not yet.

MICKEY: When did you first realize you had a big dick?

JEFF: In school, oh, yeah, in school. That is when I knew that both girls and boys were paying attention to me. I started to realize about that with my sexuality and I found out that you have to use your sexuality, that's important.

MICKEY: So you've always been aware of how good looking you are?

JEFF: It is a very nice thing. Every human being, even the Pope, is first looking at the physical appearance, it is what you see and it is first.

MICKEY: Your success has happened very quickly.

JEFF: The first year that you start is the magic year. It is when people say that you should simply have fun and enjoy. When you see someone come out of the theater and say "Gee, oh, my god, "I enjoyed that," well, I am hoping they do the same for my work. When people see me have sex and they say they want to have it, too, the same way, that is nice.

MICKEY: Is there something you want to say to fans out there?

JEFF: No matter what you do with sex—whether it's pig or romantic, you can be whatever you want—don't judge yourself by your sexuality. Your sexuality has nothing to do with your personality or your lifestyle. Whatever you want in sex you can do it without being afraid of not being a good person. Be a good person, what goes around comes around and there's no day like today.

MICKEY: You've got all the clichés down pat.

JEFF: I believe them. Whoever is judgmental—people who don't have it together—they are people not happy with themselves.

MICKEY: Anything else you want to add?

JEFF: To my fans, I wish I could fuck you all. So many fans, so little time.

The Bare Facts

Birthday: March 27, 1975
Zodiac Sign: Aries
Chinese Zodiac: Rabbit
Hair: Black
Eyes: Green
Height: 5-foot, 9-inches
Weight: 159 pounds
Cock Size: 9 1/8 inches
Favorite Color: Black and purple
Born: Argentina
Resides: West Hollywood, CA.
Workout Schedule: Two hours, three or four times a week.

Videography

The Chosen, *Falcon Studios*
Heatwave, *Falcon Studios*
Manhandlers, *Falcon Studios*
The Player, *Jocks Studios*
Stripped: Code of Conduct 1, *Falcon Studios*

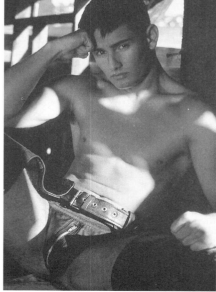

Photos courtesy: Falcon Studios

(Left) In **Stripped**, (right) In **The Chosen**

Dino Phillips

"Sure, I may have had a lot of boyfriends in porn—and those relationships didn't work—but gosh, it's hard to have a relationship, period, with anyone!"

With more than 50 video titles to his name (that we could remember), Dino Phillips groaned at the thought of doing so much porn. He's been around a lot, close to five years, and is almost holding the title as the Energizer Bunny of porn. We've known each other a long time—I've seen him through lots of boyfriends, and I've seen him on sets, in dance numbers and on stage in the play **Stripped, Barely Legal.** Friends of mine would come from out of town when he was assistant manager at one of internationally-renowned chef Wolfgang Puck's restaurants in West Hollywood, especially to see this Greek god, who became a pornstar after giving up a lucrative modeling career.

While at our favorite coffee-house, The Abbey, he looked beautiful after his workout, sporting those fluorescent green eyes and full lips, flashing his flawless smile. Since the Probe Men-in-Video Awards began he's been a perennial nominee for Most Seductive Eyes, but has lost out so far to Lukas Ridgeston and Ryan Idol—formidable opponents.

A fashion model turned pornstar

He is a smart college grad, a lean guy with a swimmer's build, and he works out for a full hour, at least, just after his favorite soap opera, "Days of Our Lives." He'll be working on his budding restaurant career and perhaps doing some writing (he's had a few erotic fictions published in past magazines), or practicing his photography or making collages.

Even at the coffeehouse he watches what he eats: no red meat or cheese, and big breakfasts. He knows how to keep fit. When he worried about his receding hairline, he cut his hair very short. Right now, he's also very popular as a stripper and regular performer for Babenet on the Internet as he continues to constantly reinvent himself in order to stay a staple in the porn world.

MICKEY: You're in my first interview book of the hottest men in gay porn; what do you think of that?

DINO: I'm honored, but it's about time! No, seriously, I feel very good about that. I've been trying to stay hot, and keep people happy. I don't want to go underground, but really it's hard to keep up and out there all the time because everybody wants new, new, new.

MICKEY: How do you stay in the business without getting overexposed?

DINO: It's hard. I lived with Chi Chi LaRue at the rancho for a while and that didn't necessarily translate into more work for me. If they've used you and used you and you're living nearby, you're not someone whose calls they return right away.

MICKEY: You have a reputation for being very dependable and being a good last minute replacement when someone else flakes for a shoot, right?

DINO: That's true, but that gets old.

MICKEY: You must get recognized a lot, do you?

DINO: Yeah, I do when I go to the gym, or in bars. It doesn't bother me; I play the pornstar role of Dino Phillips. I was recognized in the gym today—people saw me in *Bound and Gagged* magazine and said, "Hey, I saw you, you're on the cover of *Bound and Gagged*."

MICKEY: Do you go out very much?

DINO: I pretty much stay at home; I don't go out to bars much.

MICKEY: So, where can your fans run into you?

DINO: At the gym, or at a fancy new restaurant.

MICKEY: Do you think your work in adult entertainment could hurt your career in the restaurant business?

DINO: It could only enhance it. I don't see how this could hurt my plans to own my own restaurant someday.

MICKEY: You've worked with some of the best studs in the business, and perhaps the world. Which guys out there are guys you've lusted after, whom you want to work with?

DINO: Stephen Marks is very cute—someone like that type—and I would have loved to work with before he retired; and then there's that Falcon exclusive model, Drew Nolan, wow!

More recently, I like Rod Barry. I'm going to work with Rod Barry on a project with All Worlds director Mike Donner.

I would also love to work with Jim Buck. I saw him in Mike Donner's **First Time Tryers** video.

MICKEY: You perhaps have the dubious distinction of having had the most boyfriends ever in the porn industry, except for Sharon Kane, perhaps. People always ask me if the guys have trouble with relationships in this business.

DINO: Some of my boyfriends have been in porn; it doesn't matter if they're in the business. Some guys do have good relationships—like Eduardo and Sam Carson, and Sam Dixon and Jordan Young. But, mine didn't not work out for any specific reason that had to do with the industry.

MICKEY: So, let's see: you've had relationships with—

DINO: Alex Carrington, Grant Larson, Johnny Rey and Grant Wood. Sure, I may have had a lot of boyfriends in porn—and those relationships didn't work—but gosh, it's hard to have a relationship, period, with anyone! Isn't that true these days?

MICKEY: Tell me about working on **Jeff Stryker Underground**. I know you've always been a fan of his, and it was the most expensive gay porn project ever made, so I'm told.

DINO: Yeah, it was really good because I took a liking to Peter Wilder and we sort of just paired up. [Director] Gino Colbert told us to find someone we were attracted to and pair up and everybody did in this huge orgy scene on the dance floor of a local disco, and there were no soft dicks any other time. Ooops!

MICKEY: What?

DINO: I'm speaking nasty words too loud, everybody can hear, I'm embarrassed. Anyway, that was a 12 hour shift. They were filming us for 12 hours with two cameras and it took forever.

MICKEY: What was Jeff like?

DINO: Oh, he was real nice, really quiet, and he's quite a perfectionist. He wanted everything perfect and he did not want the cameras near him unless he was totally, totally hard.

MICKEY: I know you have a lot, but what are some of your favorite scenes?

DINO: Probably in the video **Happily Ever After**, the scene with Matthew Easton. And then the one with Grant Wood in **Threesome**— that was my best performance in any scene I've ever done, I think, and we started dating afterwards, so there was *something* going on there. Those two were hot scenes for me.

MICKEY: You won, at the *Adult Video News* Awards, the Best Supporting Actor honor for **Happily Ever After**, in 1997. Did that help you as a star and raise your credibility?

DINO: No, it was that awards curse. People think that prices you out of the market. I won that over a year ago and it's a curse, you don't get anything for the whole year, you have to look new and fresh again.

I've learned a lot from guys like Dallas Taylor, who reinvents himself every six months. You have to get into new things with dancing, and now the play I'm doing, and the Internet stripping.

MICKEY: You have a great following on Babenet, I hear. Do people sign on just for you?

DINO: Sure, all the time. People sign on for me and I have to do a whole bio and resume because people are constantly asking what movies do you top in or bottom in and they are constantly asking where they can find me.

MICKEY: What kind of things do they ask you to do on the Internet?

DINO: They see all the props that you have and they get rather nasty. If I'm dressed up in a baseball outfit, for example, they'll ask me to do things with the bat and tell me to stick it up my butt. And I can make it look like it does go up there because the camera is right underneath the monitor. You can fake anything.

MICKEY: Did you watch porn a lot before you were asked to do your first video?

DINO: From the moment I saw my first porn video, I loved porn. While I was coming out as gay in college I knew I someday wanted to be in front of the camera like that. My freshman year in college was the very first time that I thought about doing it and five years later, I was doing it.

MICKEY: Was it because you were an exhibitionist?

DINO: You know, I never really considered myself an exhibitionist, but I have no qualms about being naked in front people. Yet when friends of mine are over and I come out of the shower I grab a towel and put it around myself and they say, "Oh, come on, we've seen it," but I'm shy. But when I'm in front of strangers, I'm my character, and I do what people expect of this porn star character.

MICKEY: You were on plenty of covers in the past year, right?

Dino Phillips

From **Smooth Strokes**

DINO: Yeah, I made it on the cover of *Playguy* and *Honcho*, of course *Bound and Gagged*.

MICKEY: How did you get started in the business?

DINO: I was dancing at The Works nightclub, in Phoenix, Arizona, on New Year's Eve—it was turning into 1994—director Chi Chi LaRue saw me performing at the nightclub. Tyler Regan, another guy who was destined to become a pornstar, was performing with me and introduced me to Chi Chi and asked me if I wanted to do a movie. Chi Chi really wanted to meet me. He asked and I said, "Sure."

MICKEY: The first experience didn't seem to go well for you, but you did fine as you got into it, right?

DINO: Oh yeah, the second scene I did was with Jake Andrews, and I did a solo jack-off scene in **Right Hand Man** that went well. I hear a lot of guys who have a bad first experience, like me, say they never want to do it again as long as they live, but I did better the more I did. The Falcon film I did after was better. People think you just come in and have sex and get paid for it and it's easy. It's not.

MICKEY: What is it like?

DINO: Well, there's acting involved, even if it's just sex. And, you have to be a contortionist—you don't have sex like that normally. You have to move your body a certain way for the camera, keep your hands a certain way; it's not the way you ordinarily do it.

MICKEY: So then, after a few sex scenes, you moved to California?

DINO: Well, I figured if I was ever going to make it in the business, I couldn't do it with all the lumberjack dykes in Phoenix or Flagstaff. I came out and did some photo spreads.

MICKEY: What would you tell someone who wants to get into the business?

DINO: If you want to do it, you have to really want to do it. One bad time doesn't mean you can't do it. Try again.

My first movie was a horrible experience, but I like it now. The people are great. I love directors like John Rutherford, Chi Chi, and the guys are great, too. Everyone behind-the-scenes is very nice.

MICKEY: What misperceptions did you have about the sex industry that you want to tell fans about?

DINO: I was surprised at how many other companies there are in the industry, it's not just Falcon and Catalina. There're a lot of special interest companies. I've done my share of wrestling videos for B&G Videos and those are fun and quick.

MICKEY: You like doing those wrestling videos, don't you?

DINO: Sure. I wrestled in high school, and there's no cheating. You wrestle down another guy, then strip him and jack off together. I like throwing around a young guy and pinning him.

MICKEY: Any other misperceptions that you had about the industry?

DINO: The sex is very mechanical and technical, that surprised me.

MICKEY: What about the safe sex issue?

DINO: I knew it was all safe sex on the set. I've never ever seen any drugs on the set anywhere, but I know some porn actors do it off the set, but they don't push it on you.

MICKEY: What's your fans' favorite scene so far, the one the fans most ask you about?

DINO: The one I did with Buck Yeager in **The Night We Met**. And definitely another highlight was the three-way with Brandon West and Hank Hightower in **Into Leather**, as far as what people seem to remember.

MICKEY: You were a very popular fashion model in your day—why the switch?

DINO: After I graduated from Northern Arizona University in 1992, majoring in hotel management, I did some modeling and appeared in some small roles in some movies.

MICKEY: Like what?

DINO: I met "Facts of Life" star Nancy McKeon and Eric Roberts on some television movies, and did extra work in **The Getaway** and **Tombstone**. Then, I got involved with one of the top modeling agencies and was sent to Greece to do catalogues. I appeared in Adidas ads and other national ads.

MICKEY: What were the other models like?

DINO: They were gorgeous, but they were always playing it straight, talking about the girls they slept with. All the agents, photographers and makeup artists were gay but told me to straighten up my act in front of the jerky, ultra-straight guys who were models from Australia, London and New York. It was stupid.

MICKEY: You didn't like it?

DINO: It was just like Models Inc.—a lot of games, a lot of back-stabbing. I couldn't play the straight game and butch it up. I didn't want to. Guys would point out some girl on the runway and I'd look at her and feel nothing. There was nothing there.

MICKEY: Did you ever date any girls?

DINO: I did in high school, but I always knew I was attracted to guys.

MICKEY: Does your family know what you do?

DINO: My brother and sister both know, but my parents don't, they're fairly conservative. But I figure if that's the wildest thing that I do, that's OK. I never do drugs and my brother and sister still look up to me. I am the oldest, and they want to see my work, but I don't want them to really. My sister went with me to an adult bookstore in Phoenix and I showed her how many things I've done.

MICKEY: What do you want to tell your fans?

DINO: Keep renting me, and keep it up!

MICKEY: Anything else?

DINO: If you want to do this, just do it full force and don't have any qualms about what's going to happen. Because if you're constantly worried about it then it will get a hold of you for a long time.

MICKEY: That seems like a very healthy attitude.

DINO: You simply have to say "Who cares?" Don't make it such a big deal, don't make it your whole life, do it for fun. I do it for fun.

Photo courtesy: Dino Phillips

With **Rosanne**, Kurt Young, David Thompson and others.

The Bare Facts

Birthday: December 13, 1969
Zodiac Sign: Sagittarius
Chinese Zodiac: Cock
Hair: Brown
Eyes: Sparkling green
Height: 6-foot
Weight: 170 pounds
Cock Size: 8 inches
Favorite Color: Green
Born: Chicago, Ill.
Resides: Woodland Hills, Calif.
Workout Schedule: Five times a week, an hour a day.

Videography

Alex's Leather Dream, *Close-Up*
Arrested Voyeur, *Projex Video*
Beyond Punishment,
    Projex/Close-Up
Blue Nights, *Pleasure Productions*
Boys of Bel Air, *Catalina Video*
By Invitation Only, *Falcon Studios*
Chi Chi LaRue's Hard Bodies 2,
    Men of Odyssey
Come With Me, *Forum Studios*
Desert Paradise,
    Sex Video/ Video 10
Earning His Keep, *Video 10*
Face Riders, *Catalina Video*
G.V. Guide All-Star Softball
    Game, *Sabin Publishing*
Guest Services, *Catalina Video*
Happily Ever After,
    All Worlds Video
Hard Lessons, Sex Ed 2, *Minotaur*
Hard On Demand, *Video 10*
Hot Cops 2, *Centaur Films*

Hot Firemen, *Centaur Films*
Hot Springs Orgy, *Catalina Video*
How to Get a Man in Bed,
    Forum Studios
In the Mix, *All Worlds Video*
Initiation 2, *Vivid Man*
Into Leather, *Forum Studios*
Jeff Stryker Underground,
    HIS Video Gold
Keep the Tip, *Thrust Studios*
Leather Impressions,
    Midnight Men
The Night We Met, *Forum Studios*
Night With Todd Stevens,
    Vivid Man
Palm Springs Cruisin',
    Video 10/Karen Dior Productions
Please Don't Tell, *Centaur Films*
Quick Study, Sex Ed 1, *Minotaur*
Right Hand Man, *Catalina Video*
The Rush, *Spectrum Gold*
Score of Sex, *Bacchus Releasing*
Sex Toy Story 2,
    Sex Video/Video 10
The Showboys,
    Showboys Entertainment
Smooth Strokes, *Bacchus Releasing*
Spankfest, *Jet Set Productions*
Spring Fever, *Bacchus Releasing*
Star Contact, *Blue Men Productions*
Stud Fee, *Catalina Video*
Summer Love, *Sunshine Films*
Tempted, *Sex Video/Video 10*
Threesome, *Sex Video/Video 10*
Together Again, *Forum Studios*
Too Damn Big!, *Catalina Video*
Traveling Wild, *Minotaur*
The Urge, *Vivid Man*
Watering Game, *Close Up*
Wet Warehouse, *Forum Studios*

Steve Rambo

"I have no problem with getting a hard-on. Keeping it up is very natural for me. The only problem is that I get so turned on, I have to refrain from cumming so quickly and right away."

He's slick yet sweet, hot and hip, nasty and yet very nice. Steve Rambo comes across on the screen as a scary, handsome man who would easily intimidate anyone who comes near him, but the reality is, he's truly a nice guy. And just like his changing demeanor, he has many different looks—shaved, unshaved, pierced or not, long hair and short hair.

He's an exclusive Catalina model, so that's where you'll find most of his videos. He does it in the woods with Tony Bracco, after some heated phone sex in **Mountain Jock** , he yanks off solo in **Right Hand Man**, and Rip Stone just about rips him apart in **Tainted Love**. He's in some of Catalina's past greats, such as the leather offering **Initiation**, the lavish **Cat Men Do**, and stars in one of the best videos of the year, **Catalinaville**, which features him in a wild, and memorable, cross-country chase.

The 5-foot-9-inch, 200-pound stud with the 32 inch waist, lounges casually in his West Hollywood apartment as we talk about mutual friends and what nasty, kinky and revealing outfit he will wear to the upcoming gay awards show. His chest is 47 inches and his arms are 17. Want more dimensions? You can buy them outright with the complete Steve Rambo Butt & Dong, one of the most bizarre dildos ever made, designed by Catalina—you can give it up the butt and take it at the same time. The dildo is bendable, but stiff; the balls are in little, egg-shaped, rolly scrotum sacks. It's probably as close to fucking and being fucked by Steve Rambo as many of us will ever get.

He's been gay all his life—he just knew it—and his parents not only know that he's a rising pornstar, they've also asked if they could watch one of his videos with him!

Steve Rambo at the *Gay Erotic Video Awards* holding his trophy

MICKEY: You must be getting a lot of jokes about the dildo?

STEVE: Oh sure, it still is very fun. At first it didn't bother me, but then when I saw it in a package in a bookstore with my picture on it, it threw me for a loop. Everyone jokes about it.

MICKEY: And they say?

STEVE: What they tell me is how they like to fuck and get fucked at the same time. I had one guy tell me the other day, "You gave me a blow job this morning," and I'm thinking, "Hmmm, I don't remember that they got an impression of my mouth."

MICKEY: So you had to stick your hard-on into some plastic goo for awhile?

STEVE: We were doing it at some rubber plant in the Valley, and I had to work it up and get it hard. Then, three Latino women came out from the back to peel it off for me, and I thought, "Hey, it's going down already, where are the three Latino men?"

MICKEY: You must be excited for the world to see **Catalinaville**?

STEVE: Yes, I think it's going to be my best role ever.

MICKEY: And does that mean we'll see more of you getting involved in stuff behind the scenes, like directing or writing?

STEVE: Yes—well, writing—definitely. While that shoot was going on for **Catalinaville** I would keep watching how things get done and I decided I'd get more involved with the storyline and do more behind-the-scenes work and maybe more writing. What I'd like to do before I retire is become a director.

MICKEY: You also have aspirations to go into mainstream acting, right?

STEVE: Yeah, I think I'd like to. If I'm hired for a soap opera, I may not direct a porn video, but we'll see.

MICKEY: Would you try to hide your porn past?

STEVE: I know you can't. If anything would come up, then I would say, "Oh, you think that's dirt? Yeah, yeah OK, I did it." And then so what? I don't think people care anymore.

MICKEY: What do you think about being part of this book?

STEVE: It's cool and great being in your book. I love being in this business and in all these magazines and books because, in a way, this sort of thing gets me out of my shell. I was living in small-town Rochester, New York, and now in some circles I'm a star.

MICKEY: And how did you get into the business?

STEVE: Well, it's a funny story—my roommate got a job at a photo studio where he was filing things, and I'd come to pick him up from work sometimes and the guys at work would see me. He would also hire his house out occasionally to do shoots for Catalina videos.

MICKEY: Yeah, and?

STEVE: Well, one day, one of the models dropped out and they were pretty desperate and they went to the guy who owned the house and said, "Do you think he would try it?" And then they asked me and I said, "I don't know if I want to." I mean, I knew I could fill in, but I didn't really know.

MICKEY: What convinced you?

STEVE: Well, the money helped, and I said I'd give it a try and I did it right then and there.

MICKEY: What movie was that?

STEVE: I believe that was **Hot Properties**.

MICKEY: And that opened the doors to Catalina—as an exclusive model, of course.

STEVE: Of course.

MICKEY: So, the first time you had sex in front of a camera: were you nervous?

STEVE: I felt like I could handle it if I tried it, and I realized after the first time that it was something I could do and I enjoyed it.

MICKEY: You've worked with every Catalina director haven't you? They're all great guys.

STEVE: Yes, Chet Thomas, Brad Austin, who was my first director and Josh Eliot, and I've worked with Chi Chi LaRue, too. They all make you feel very much at home. They're very good at making you feel comfortable in a first-time situation.

MICKEY: Did you watch your first video?

STEVE: I have no trouble with it. In fact, I own every single one of my videos.

MICKEY: Was there any misconception of what it was going to be like in the adult industry before you got in it?

STEVE: Not really, I wasn't very familiar with how it worked, but I have a lot of friends in the business. Harold Ramsey is a great photographer and he has sort of taken me under his wing and represents me like an agent.

I never had any of those odd ideas that the industry is filled with drugs and unprotected or forced sex. That's totally untrue because I knew so people in the industry beforehand and I've never seen that before.

MICKEY: Anything else?

STEVE: Sure, there was the safe sex issue. I was concerned about safe sex and how much of it was done on the sets, and what I found out was incredible. People are very, very safe and they don't push you to do anything risky. There's always protection around.

MICKEY: What's the worst part about doing a film?

STEVE: It's the stop and go; there's a lot of it. It's not as easy as it looks when you're spending half the day on one scene. I have to get into the rhythm.

MICKEY: And then of course there's the hard-on problems.

STEVE: Well, I have no problem with getting a hard-on. Keeping it up is very natural for me. The only problem is that I get so turned on, I have to refrain from cumming so quickly and right away.

MICKEY: How do you deal with that?

STEVE: Very simply. I just tell them that I want to break for a bit and I go off and relax. I do that just to get back into the scene. It's easy to get real excited.

MICKEY: What scene has been the most fun for you to shoot?

STEVE: The hottest scene I've done is definitely in **Hot Springs Orgy**. That was with Max Grand. We were out in front in the patio area and I was sitting on top of him. That was hot.

MICKEY: And aren't you getting into the leather thing, too?

STEVE: I just finished another product from Catalina that I think is going to be called **Initiation**. It features me with this leather that I'm wearing.

MICKEY: You've also got a new look now don't you?

STEVE: Yeah, I used to shave my chest just before a shoot, but I don't like to do that because there's that stubble that comes in just the next day. Then, I grew a goatee and cut off my whole head of hair.

MICKEY: Readers say they want guys natural-looking, with lots of hair.

STEVE: That's what I've been saying all along, too. The last thing I'll ever do again is to try a waxing on my chest before the scene. It was like trying to pull a Band-aid off a hairy arm, but this time imagine it's your chest hairs. And the lady who was doing the waxing had the wax too hot and she apologized after.

MICKEY: Are there any funny moments you had on the set?

STEVE: Sure, one time when Chi Chi was on the set—he always makes me laugh—but one time, I was in a scene in Palm Springs for the **Palms Springs Orgy** video and I backed into a cactus.

MICKEY: Naked?

STEVE: Totally naked.

MICKEY: Ouch!

STEVE: That's what I said.

MICKEY: Part of the hazards of working in the industry.

STEVE: Anyway, when someone else did the same thing we ended up moving the scene.

MICKEY: Who has been the favorite guy you've worked with so far?

STEVE: I'd have to say Max Grand. He's fun and gives it his all.

MICKEY: Did you ever have a sexual encounter with someone who you weren't into?

STEVE: Sure, the guys who are gay-for-pay. There was one video I did, I think it was **Roommate**, where we had sex in the kitchen and you could just tell he wasn't into me.

MICKEY: What do you think of the guys who are gay-for-pay, in other words, they are straight, or claim to be, but are really bisexual or gay but are too afraid to admit it?

STEVE: I think they're phonies. They sit there talking about their girlfriends and have to look at women's magazines to get hard and they give lousy head.

MICKEY: They do, do they?

STEVE: Yeah, there's no suction when a straight guy gives you head. I like it powerful. If they give me attitude or something like that, it's hard for me to stay hard, if you know what I mean. You can tell in certain videos, just watch them. The straight guys always just have their mouths opened. No suction. Once I even grabbed the guy at the back of the head and said "Suck it, dude," because I couldn't keep a hard-on.

MICKEY: Do you have a specific idea you would like to write?

STEVE: I'd like to write a few scripts someday for myself. I have some ideas.

MICKEY: Like what? Tell us your fantasy.

STEVE: I like guys in nice suits. That's a fantasy of mine. I think of a New York City skyrise and a guy working late, and I'm thinking it would be neat to play a clean-up guy—undoing this guy's suit and tie and shirt and going at it right there on his desk. Then, a prim and proper board of directors have a meeting on the same table.

MICKEY: No doubt with some unusual stains left behind.

STEVE: Of course. That would be great.

MICKEY: Did you watch porno before you got into it?

STEVE: I watched it all the time. I never paid attention to names per se, but videos are what helped me come out. I grew up in Rochester, New York, up state, and we only had bookstores, so I rented some and took them home.

MICKEY: Did your parents know you did that?

STEVE: Well, Dad always tried to keep his stash of women's magazines hidden, but I would find it and look at the men in it, not the women.

MICKEY: Had you ever been attracted to women?

STEVE: Once. I thought I was in love with her, and when I had sex with her finally, I said, "Well I'm not gay then." But then I tried it again with a man, and I thought, "Yuck, I'm not into this women thing," and the rest is history.

MICKEY: When did you realize you had a huge cock and guys were checking you out?

STEVE: When I had just turned 17 I was working out a lot in the gym and guys were always looking at me. Straight ones, too. That was the problem, I was always too shy to ask any of the cute guys out because I was nervous they would be straight.

MICKEY: What a shame.

STEVE: It is though, because there were these cute guys I hung around with who now in retrospect were offering me the opportunities for sex but I always ignored it. Now those suckers are married.

MICKEY: And they're probably sneaking out and renting your videos.

STEVE: (*Laughs*) Yeah, probably. But I don't care who knows. My parents know.

MICKEY: What?! That's a story in itself.

STEVE: We were at the dinner table in New York around the holidays and that was after I had made about seven videos. And in the middle of dinner, my dad's wife answers the phone and says "No kidding" and "I don't believe it" a lot of times while clutching her breast— another relative had seen the tapes. So she gets off the phone and turns to me and asks, "Did you make porn videos in L.A.?"

MICKEY: What did you do?

STEVE: I didn't deny it, but there were kids at the table. We talked after supper and they were really cool about it. They said, "You go do what you want to do" and they let me be the starving artist.

MICKEY: That's pretty cool.

STEVE: What's more strange is that they asked if they could watch one of the videos with me. I freaked and said, "NO WAY!" and they said they were going to rent one on their own.

MICKEY: I could just see your dad looking through the gay section of a video store telling people he's looking for his son.

STEVE: He'd probably send her, my step-mother.

MICKEY: How did you make them think it was OK that you did porn?

STEVE: I explained that in a way it was acting and that I like it. I do read many of the reviews of the videos and in many of them reviewers seem to say that they like my acting. A professional dancer friend of mine showed me the magazine *Dramalogue* and I'm going to go through it and go in for mainstream auditions.

MICKEY: That's great.

STEVE: I don't feel totally nervous about going out in front of the camera, I mean when you're naked doing it, what could be worse than that?

MICKEY: Any other scenes that you've done or co-stars that you are pretty wild about?

STEVE: Funny that you use the word wild, because another one of my most favorite scenes is in **Ranger in the Wild**, and every time I watch that video that scene gets me hot. It's with Daryl Brock; he's very nice and knows how to work it.

MICKEY: You're one of the older guys in adult video.

STEVE: I started later, and I don't look as old as I am, so I'm not ashamed of telling my age. I was born in 1957.

MICKEY: And let's not leave this hanging—did your family ever get into a video store and see one of your videos?

STEVE: That's a funny story. My stepmother was in a store and used my dad's card—he has the same name as I do—and the clerk asked if that was Steve Rambo.

He took her back to the back room and showed her all the titles I've been in and she rented **Night of the Living Bi Dolls**.

MICKEY: Hey, I'm in that one, too, but they wouldn't let me take my clothes off.

STEVE: She called me up and said, "Hi, Mr. Steve Rambo," and said she watched it up until the sex part and hasn't gotten to that part, but they laughed a lot and said they liked my acting. It still amazes me; it's very cool. She's pretty cool. Of course, she's only a year older than me, my dad re-married young.

MICKEY: Is it unusual to you that guys are now demanding more of the older, rougher look in their videos?

STEVE: No, that's definitely the trend. When I go do my shows in different cities they like my hairy chest, my goatee; they say they don't like the kewpie, shaved little muscle-boys anymore. I didn't realize that that's what is being reflected in what porn fans want. I came into business at the right time.

MICKEY: What kind of guy do you go for?

STEVE: For a relationship with me, I look for someone with a swimmer's build; he has to be not too hairy, slender and has to be somebody who I can hug and squeeze tight.

MICKEY: So you like to dominate a guy?

STEVE: Yeah. I also lean toward Hispanic guys, like that guy from Falcon, Mike Lamas.

MICKEY: And are you getting recognized out and about town?

STEVE: Yes. I've done enough videos that I'll see guys take double looks at me and then come up close and say, "Did you used to do videos?" And I say I still do. I don't mind it when people come up to talk to me.

MICKEY: They'll also whisper behind your back.

STEVE: I hate when they do that. They might as well come up to me and talk. I'm a pretty easygoing guy.

MICKEY: What would you say to someone wanting to get into porn?

STEVE: I would say you have to be open-minded, and if you're going to freak out the first time someone notices you, or you'll regret it, then you're not at ease with it.

The Bare Facts

Birthday: November 25, 1957
Zodiac Sign: Sagittarius
Chinese Zodiac: Cock
Hair: Brown
Eyes: Brown
Height: 5-foot, 9 1/2-inches
Weight: 200 pounds
Cock Size: 8 1/2 inches
Favorite Color: Blue
Born: Rochester, NY.
Resides: Palm Springs, Calif.
Workout Schedule: 2 1/2 hours a day, five days a week.

Videography

Ace in Your Face, *Catalina Video*
Cat Men Do, *Catalina Video*
Catalinaville, *Catalina Video*
Chicago Erection Company,
 Catalina Video
Detour,*Catalina Video*
Dudes, *Stallion Video/Leisure
 Time Entertainment*
Hell Bent For Leather,
 Catalina Video
Hot Properties,*Catalina Video*
Hot Springs Orgy, *Catalina Video*
**International Male Leather
 Initiation**, *Catalina Video*
Logjammer, *Catalina Video*
Mountain Jock, *Catalina Video*
Night of the Living Bi Dolls,
 Catalina Video
Nutt Crackers, *Catalina Video*

Palm Springs Weekend,
 Catalina Video
Priority Male, *Catalina Video*
Ranger in the Wild,*Catalina Video*
Right Hand Man,*Catalina Video*
The Roommate, *Catalina Video*
Street Boyz, *Catalina Video*
Studio Tricks, *Catalina Video*
Tainted Love, *Catalina Video*

Steve Rambo, Catalina Video exclusive

Photo courtesy: Catalina Video

Scott Randsome

"I do watch my own videos, only sometimes. I'd get off watching how turned on I was, but I'd also watch to see how comfortable I was, how I looked, more of the technical aspect."

I t was his birthday when I landed some time with the ever-popular Scott Randsome. He was heading out to a fantastic magic show in Las Vegas, wearing a black, tight, shoulder-hugging tank top and even closer hip-hugging slacks and looking ever so cute. Randsome is a muscle-stud fantasy man. He's kind to his fans, loves signing autographs and is very demure among admirers.

At famed director Chi Chi LaRue's birthday party last year he remained shyly off in a corner with friends, seemingly in awe of fellow stars he'd only ever seen on video. Scott is as courteous, simple and humpy as he comes across on screen, but he thinks he is a bit more friendly in person.

He does land some juicy roles. He was a cowboy in Studio 2000's hit **Mavericks**, took part in a steamy jack-off in the award-winning spoof **Sunsex Boulevard**, by Catalina, became a dream date (and box coverboy, in Vivid's **The Personals**, and played a sleazy interviewer getting the scoop from Ryan Block in HIS Video Gold's **Fame & Flesh**.

He loved playing the badboy surfer bodybuilder who helps Gianfranco maul Chad Conners on the beach in Studio 2000's **Riptide!** In **Wanted**, from Catalina, he screwed two award-winning, famed bottom-boys Johnny Rey and Tim Barnett. He's also topped both sides of the porn industry's hottest couple, Jake Andrews and Karl Bruno—Andrews in an oily auto mechanic's fuck in Jocks' **Greased Up**, and Bruno in **Riptide!** and **Total Corruption 2**, from HIS Video Gold. In that one, they're fucking in the woods when overzealous cop Blade Thompson stumbles across them. Another highlight is Donnie Russo getting his face fucked by Scott's thick massive cock in his best showing: **The Summer of**

In **Sunsex Boulevard**

Scott Randsome, by Catalina. Also, for those who like raw wrestling, he's got some fantastic amateur-like videos coming out via Can-Am Productions.

He's got no pretensions, what you see is what you get with Scott—all muscle-bound mounds of him.

MICKEY: Thank you for taking the time to let me interview you on such a busy day.

SCOTT: No problem, I always have time for you.

MICKEY: So, it's your birthday—Happy Birthday—and you're out celebrating with the guys.

SCOTT: Yeah, it's going to be a mellow night.

MICKEY: You don't seem afraid to tell us your age like other guys in the business usually are.

SCOTT: Nah, it's no big deal. I'm still young: I think I've got a few more years in me before I start worrying about my age.

MICKEY: It's amazing how you've taken the business by storm in a very short time. You had only a few videos out when you were already considered an A-list pornstar.

SCOTT: Thanks, I've been pretty lucky.

MICKEY: Is there anything that you would have done differently, looking back on it now?

SCOTT: I don't know, it might have been a little different if I planned on staying in the business a little bit more; I'm not in it for the long term, I don't think.

MICKEY: Why don't you think you're going to be in the business very long?

SCOTT: I don't know, I'm realistic about it. I know it is something that wouldn't last: it's a short-lived job.

MICKEY: So you're not very serious about it.

SCOTT: I think of it as kind of a hobby.

MICKEY: Did you get that advice from fellow stars?

SCOTT: I know people in the business, and took my cues from people like Scott Baldwin, Derek Cruise and Phil Bradley. They were friends of mine.

MICKEY: They're all big names—or were—in adult entertainment over the past few years.

SCOTT: Yeah, they're great guys.

MICKEY: And, ironically enough, they all have great bubble butts like yours.

SCOTT: Yeah.

MICKEY: Do you know how many people are going to be disappointed to hear that you're not planning on staying in the video market for very much longer?

SCOTT: I'll be in it long enough fpr people to enjoy me. Maybe another year or two more, that's all. Different people get in it for different reasons, you know. Some people get in it for the longevity of it, they're doing it for a career.

MICKEY: And what is Scott Randsome doing it for?

SCOTT: It seemed like a fun, good way to earn some money.

MICKEY: And it is.

SCOTT: Yes, it is very much.

MICKEY: What do you do with that money?

SCOTT: I consider the bucks I make in this as travel money. I put it aside in an account that I use for seeing the country; I like to travel.

MICKEY: Where have you been?

SCOTT: In the last year and a half I've been to New York, Cancun, Mexico, Ohio, Maui, Florida and Texas.

MICKEY: I know you're also doing appearances in some of those places.

SCOTT: Yeah, it's always nice to mix business with pleasure.

MICKEY: Do you have friends in the business?

SCOTT: Some, yes, but it's hard to make too many friends and have one or two other things in your life as well.

MICKEY: Where are you living now?

SCOTT: In Orange County, Laguna Niguel, and I grew up in Torrance.

MICKEY: A very conservative part of California.

SCOTT: Yes, it is. That's where I work out and train.

MICKEY: How did you get into the business?

SCOTT: I started to compete as a bodybuilder as a teenager.

MICKEY: Wow, that's great.

SCOTT: I got picked to be in a Fox Calendar, and that's the first time I modeled for anyone, and I liked it.

MICKEY: Of course that wasn't naked at the time because you were still a teenager. Did it take a while for them to convince you to do it?

SCOTT: There was some mild persuasion, but they offered me $1,000 for a nude calendar as soon as I turned 21.

MICKEY: Then, they convinced you?

SCOTT: Yeah, first it was to do a calendar, then it was to do the sex. Finally, it was Josh Eliot at Catalina Video who kept trying to convince me to do my first movie.

MICKEY: He's a great director.

SCOTT: Sure is—I was 21 and a half and I guess I was ready to do it.

MICKEY: That movie was **Sunsex Boulevard**, their spoof on **Sunset Boulevard** that picked up the Best Sex Comedy at the *Gay Video Guide* Awards, right?

SCOTT: That's the one.

MICKEY: How was it the first time?

SCOTT: In front of the cameras, it was scary. I was nervous and scared at first with all the lights and the camera and five or six people watching and waiting for me to get hard.

MICKEY: That was new for you?

SCOTT: Well, usually when I had sex before that there was only one other person there. (*Laughs*)

MICKEY: Did you watch porno before you got in them yourself?

SCOTT: Sure, but I never did see myself as someone who would be good in a porn role. What do you think?

MICKEY: You certainly fit the bill in my book. Some guys don't ever watch themselves on video—have you?

SCOTT: When I first started I did watch myself, just to see what I was doing right or wrong. Now I watch how the movie is made, but I don't watch as much and I haven't seen all my movies yet.

MICKEY: I guess it can be awkward?

SCOTT: It's awkward.

MICKEY: Did you ever get off watching yourself?

SCOTT: I do watch my own videos, only sometimes. I'd get off watching how turned on I was, but I'd also watch to see how comfortable I was, how I looked, more of the technical aspect. Was I in good shape? Could I be a few pounds lighter. Stuff like that.

MICKEY: That's important.

SCOTT: It's important to look like I was having a good time.

MICKEY: Do you have a favorite scene that you've done so far?

SCOTT: There was that hot scene with Jake Andrews, he was a great guy to work with, a big man, all hairy, great muscles.

MICKEY: That would have been the auto mechanic scene in Jocks' **Greased Up**?

SCOTT: That's right. Jake was a total sweetheart.

MICKEY: Anyone else that you really like working with?

Scott Randsome

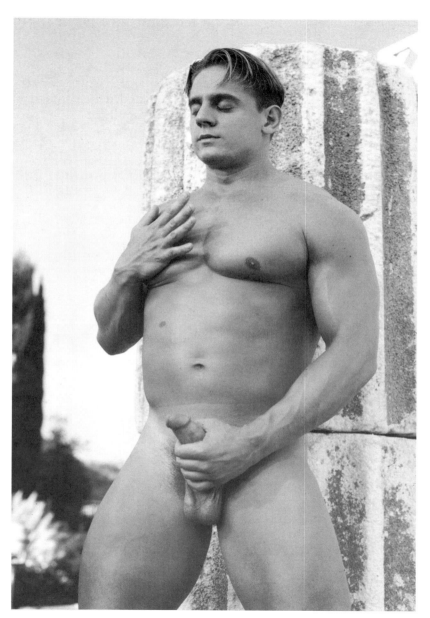

Photo courtesy: Catalina Videos

Don't let the sun go down, in **Sunsex Boulevard**

SCOTT: I'm doing those wrestling videos, they're a lot of fun. I like working with Christian Fox, Jake and Tom Katt. Those are my favorites so far.

MICKEY: Those wrestling videos are quite different. You don't even have sex in them.

SCOTT: Yeah, but they're really erotic. You have to have a great body to be in them. The guys I've done them with all have great bodies, and that's a real turn-on. The wrestling scenes are like sex fights.

MICKEY: And what are you like by day, when you're not Scott Randsome?

SCOTT: I'm just a normal, ordinary college student.

MICKEY: I'll bet. Do you consider yourself gay or bisexual?

SCOTT: I've stopped labeling myself. I don't know what I am.

MICKEY: Have you ever had a boyfriend?

SCOTT: So far I've never found a guy I would settle down with as a boyfriend. I wouldn't rule it out. It's not that I couldn't.

MICKEY: But you are still attracted to girls, too?

SCOTT: I found that I'm universally attracted to both, to all kinds of people.

MICKEY: That's cool. So I don't see you much out in the West Hollywood club scene.

SCOTT: No, I don't know the West Hollywood scene. I find it sort of weird.

MICKEY: You're more into other things?

SCOTT: I spend a lot of my time on body building. I'm getting better and better at it.

MICKEY: What's your workout schedule?

SCOTT: To stay toned it's three or four times a week for an hour to an hour-and-a-half a day. That's just to stay toned.

MICKEY: It's more when you're in competition?

SCOTT: Sure.

MICKEY: And your diet? Do you have a special diet?

SCOTT: Yes, I'm very very conscious about eating healthy, and I stay away from butter and sauces.

MICKEY: What are your stats now?

SCOTT: I'm 5-foot-8-inches tall and weigh about 180 now. My arms are 17 inches and I have a 30-inch waist, my legs are 25 inches and my chest is 46 inches.

MICKEY: Sounds good, but you left out one statistic.

SCOTT: What?

MICKEY: Cock size?

SCOTT: Oh yeah, that's 8 and 3/4 inches.

MICKEY: Yes. Now I hear that you're often dancing in gay clubs throughout Florida?

SCOTT: Yes, I like going to Fort Lauderdale.

MICKEY: Does your family know about the videos?

SCOTT: They don't know about the porno business, but they do know a little bit here and there. They know about the gay nightclub circuit and they know about the calendar, I've showed that to them. I have not over-divulged.

MICKEY: And what are you studying in college?

SCOTT: Real estate. I want to get my real estate license.

MICKEY: You like making money, then?

SCOTT: Even when I was a kid, even at 15, I was fundraising for charities and stuff like that.

MICKEY: Do you have a favorite director?

SCOTT: Not really a totally favorite, but Chi Chi LaRue makes me feel really comfortable on the set. There's an attitude of how you can be on the set that makes you more comfortable to perform.

MICKEY: Everyone seems to say that about Chi Chi's sets. What gives?

SCOTT: Well, you've been on Chi Chi's sets. It's the way he talks to you. Everything is positive and he's easy going and everything feels real simple.

MICKEY: Tell me a fantasy of yours that you haven't yet fulfilled on video.

SCOTT: Maybe a hot guy and a girl, that might be the ticket. Maybe me and Tom Katt doing a bisexual scene in a video, that would be great.

MICKEY: Well, there haven't been many good bisexual videos out in a long time, maybe someone will get an idea for that!

SCOTT: Hope so.

MICKEY: How are you when fans come up to you and recognize you?

SCOTT: I'm real nice to people when they come up to me when I'm alone. It's a lot different when I'm with a group of friends because it gets awkward and sometimes the people I'm with don't know that side of me. I'm still nice and polite and admit who I am.

MICKEY: Right, I know some guys in the adult business who won't admit it to fans, they say, "What are you talking about?" or "You got the wrong guy" and that could be mean.

SCOTT: Yeah. That's not very nice. I don't do that.

MICKEY: How are you in relationships?

SCOTT: I'm a more personal person than I am in videos. I always feel like if you treat a person well, they'll treat you well in return.

MICKEY: And is there something special you'd like to tell your fans?

SCOTT: That's the best message I could give them all.

MICKEY: What would you change about the business if you could?

SCOTT: The money. I think actors should get paid more.

MICKEY: In what way?

SCOTT: Well, if the product is more heavily publicized, like me getting on the box or something, then a star should get a percentage of the tapes.

MICKEY: Then you'd be really rich.

SCOTT: Yeah.

The Bare Facts

Birthday: July 26, 1972
Zodiac Sign: Leo
Chinese Zodiac: Rat
Hair: Blond
Eyes: Blue
Height: 5 foot, 8 inches
Weight: 180
Cock Size: 8 3/4 inches
Favorite Color: Royal blue
Born: Torrance, Calif.
Resides: Laguna Niguel, Calif.
Workout Schedule: One to one-and-a-half hours a day, three or four times a week.

Videography

Fun in the Sun, *Catalina*
Sex in the Great Outdoors 4,
   Catalina
Fame & Flesh, *HIS Video Gold*
Catalina Weekend, *Catalina*
Greased Up, *Jocks*
Manhattan Skyline,
   HIS Video Gold
Mavericks, *Studio 2000*
Personals, *Vivid Man*
Riptide!, *Studio 2000*
Secret Sex 3, *Catalina*
Sunsex Boulevard, *Catalina*
Summer of Scott Randsome,
   Catalina
Total Corruption 2: One Night in Jail, *HIS Video Gold*
Wanted, *Catalina*

Photos courtesy: Jocks Studios

Photos courtesy: Catalina Video

(Left) from **Greased Up**, (right) from **Jocks**

Tanner Reeves

"The best thing I ever did in my life was doing porn. I had low self-esteem, I didn't like myself or my body; and now people I don't know think of me as very attractive and sexual—that's so weird to me."

The last I heard, he was dead. But, there he was, sitting in my backyard with a huge buffed chest and a winning, shiny smile, willing to give me his first interview after one of the biggest comebacks ever in gay porn—a comeback from death! He's always been the charmer of the adult industry, always a professional, always dependable, always cute, always a friend. No doubt he's one of this past year's greatest success stories, and he's very well deserving of a spot in this book, even though he's one of the first people to say that he's not and never has been—and never aspires to be—a superstar in porn.

When I first heard of his accident, it was one of many tragic moments that hit the porn world in recent years. By all accounts, Tanner Reeves was dead—at the least, his porn career was most definitely dead. He was hit by a truck while riding his bicycle on Pico Boulevard, not far from the 20th Century Fox Studios lot. He was dragged by the truck, he was knocked 100 feet and landed on his face, he may have to get an arm amputated—spine-chilling details and rumors flooded the gossip magazines of West Hollywood. For the most part, they were accurate, and for a year I was the only person in porn whom Tanner talked to during his recovery.

Tanner was just about to start a new life by moving to Hawaii to start a new business there. Contrary to an overzealous writer who wrote that his arm was "cut off!" he had his elbow practically rebuilt because of the accident, and will face years of reconstructive surgery. He may never regain the full use of his right hand, but he's "doing as well as can be" and he is swinging into a major comeback with companies just itching to get him back.

From **Risky Sex**

In the court proceedings involving the accident, his lawyer interviewed me in order to testify that Tanner Reeves was in fact a viable, important name in the adult porn world. There's no question he was, and is, and I was ready to be the objective source of that information.

Fans are writing about what a delight it is to hear Tanner is back on top after the tragic accident. With 28 chipped bone fragments in his arm healing slowly, he's getting some of the feeling in his arm back and he's getting money from the company of the truck that hit him and flipped him down the street. Ironically, he looks better than he did before the accident, and he says he feels better, too. He's quite happy with the way things are going as he is on the mend—physically, and with his porn career after a two-year absence.

It proves that the porn revision of the old adage works: "Nice porn-stars don't finish last, when they *cum* back, they do it a lot more force-fully!"

MICKEY: Obviously, we have to start with the accident. You were on your way out of the business when this accident happened weren't you?

TANNER: Actually, I was going to take a bit of time off.

MICKEY: Not totally retire.

TANNER: No, not yet. I had saved up my money and it was a plan for two years for me. I wanted to work with tourists in Hawaii. I was going to commute, come back into town every couple of months and do a few flicks and then go back to Maui.

MICKEY: People were making it sound like you were sneaking off and leaving all your friends behind and just disappearing.

TANNER: Not true. I really liked the people I met in the adult industry and I liked those I was going into business with.

MICKEY: Most of your stuff was already in Hawaii.

TANNER: Yes, I sold my car, I did the big garage sale and most of my stuff was shipped off already. I was going to partly own this dive shop and we had a place already picked in Maui. My friend was the primary investor and we would have dive equipment, snorkels and jet skis. I was saving up money I made from the adult business for it. It was my long-range plan finally coming to fruition.

MICKEY: Wow, you had it all set up?

TANNER: Oh yeah, I already had the apartment there for a year before I was going out. I know how to dive and snorkel and I was really familiar with the islands and where to go and I already had great contacts with some of the hotels there. We were already set to take groups out.

MICKEY: Is this still an option for you?

TANNER: If I heal well enough and can swim OK, I will do it. I may get a good enough settlement to open my own shop all by myself, which would be fun.

MICKEY: This was literally your last day in Los Angeles before you had the accident?

TANNER: It was the second to the last day. It was on Pico Boulevard and Overland Avenue, near the Westside Pavilion Shopping Center. I was riding my bike to the beach because it was my last time here.

MICKEY: So how did the accident happen?

TANNER: They were laying pavement and the city had moved the bike path to the opposite side of the street into oncoming traffic. I was riding my bike near City Bank and a delivery truck pulled out from a place where it shouldn't have been. The driver wasn't using the delivery space where he was supposed to have been. He tried to gun it out of the parking lot and he just nailed me, just nailed me. He completely broadsided me.

MICKEY: Did you see it coming, did you see him coming?

TANNER: I saw him just out of the corner of my eye. I saw him come right out from between two buildings.

My bike went under the truck and it threw me and I flew four lanes into oncoming traffic.

MICKEY: Ouch!

TANNER: I was pretty hamburgered up. I went up in the air and it popped the shoulder and blew out the elbow and the hand itself broke back, it broke and severed and ripped this and cut that. I don't remember too much of the aftermath. I could not figure out why my hand had no feeling and how my hand snapped so far back.

MICKEY: Did you think this was the end?

TANNER: I really don't even know what I thought. It was so quick. I do remember coming down. I remember thinking that I was flying. I saw myself coming down and flying four lanes. I saw the pavement coming toward me and witnesses said I did three cartwheels in the air. I came down and bit it.

MICKEY: Do you still have nightmares about this?

TANNER: You know what's funny is, yes, I do, but I have a fear of front tires of trucks. I remember seeing a dump truck wheel coming at me when I was laying in the street. It came so close to running me over again after I was hit. I haven't been able to drive, but when I am in a car now, I always look at front truck tires. I knew I was going to get it.

MICKEY: They obviously did stop in time.

TANNER: Oh, yeah. The next thing I knew it was a few days later. I had already given up my apartment, I had no furniture. They told me that I needed surgery and physical therapy and they told me it was going to take one or two years and I said, "Oh, god, no, it can't be." Everything was planned for me to leave, this couldn't happen.

MICKEY: You were going to lose that arm for awhile there, right?

TANNER: At one point it got really infected, and what happened is that the initial set that was done was malforming. It was so inflamed they couldn't cast it and it turned black and blue and cut off the circulation. It was basically rotting. They had to snap it again and put in a new brace. I had five casts in 15 months. Right now I have really bad arthritis and tendonitis and will have that for the rest of my life.

MICKEY: What kept you going through all this?

TANNER: The fact that I wasn't ready to go back to being a wallflower. Up until I was doing movies, I had been in L.A. 10 years and knew maybe two people. I was shy. When I started doing films and all that, it brought me out of my shell. Before that I was reclusive.

MICKEY: Will you ever be the same again?

TANNER: Right now, I'm careful, but I lift weights and I'm in constant therapy.

MICKEY: It sounds awful. But you made a great comeback. So why did you want to do porn in the first place?

TANNER: It's a way for me to do and be everything I wanted to do and be.

MICKEY: Are you still getting recognized?

TANNER: All the time. Somebody asked me for an autograph at the Buzz Coffee House last week and then yesterday at the Sunset Boulevard Laemle Theaters. How funny that people ask for that. People thought I was gone because they heard about the accident. I was so incredibly angry about the accident. I thought long and hard while I was laid up.

MICKEY: That's right, we talked a bit.

TANNER: You honestly are the only person I talked to throughout the year. We talked every couple of months.

You were also the person who mentioned to me that I should do a comeback. You said, "Tanner, when you're ready, do it because people miss you and still want to see you." And I swear to god, I'm not buttering you up, but that was the deciding point, Mickey. When you showed me letters that people wrote and said "fans miss you"—for Mickey Skee to say that, it meant a lot.

MICKEY: Aw shucks, I'm embarrassed now.

TANNER: When people see me on the street now, they say, "I thought your arm was cut off and you were all beat up," and I say, "That was a year ago."

MICKEY: And why make a comeback?

TANNER: There was no better way to say "I'm here." In a town that judges you by what you wear, how you look, what you drive, it was my way of fighting back. I hate the whole West Hollywood crowd that makes me feel bad about myself, and those are the same people who talk bad about everyone else.

MICKEY: Who gave you the best advice about the porn world?

TANNER: It was director Chi Chi LaRue who told me I could go and do one video or two and I would be considered somebody who did porn. Or I could be someone who did a lot and go from being porn trash to porn actor. I don't consider myself to be a pornstar. I don't think I'm a pornstar, I'm in 100 videos, I think. I don't know how many.

MICKEY: I counted 107.

TANNER: Wow, gee. I see myself on boxcovers, especially recently, and I still have videos everywhere and have videos coming out to this day. How did all this happen? I keep asking myself that. I did exactly what I wanted to do.

People say "he's not a pornstar, he doesn't do scenes for $2,000," but I don't feel badly about myself about not doing scenes for that amount of money. I'm flattered that people want me to do it and I am asked to do it. It's not about the money at all.

MICKEY: What ultimately made you think you could have sex in front of people?

TANNER: When I turned 31, I thought "there's got to be more than working in a hotel," I had low self-esteem. It wasn't so much about being gay, it was about me being me.

I grew up in a little white trash town in Texas—I grew up in foster homes and left them when I turned 13—and was on my own after that. I kept being told that I was nothing and that my parents didn't want me and that I didn't get adopted and I was never going to amount to anything.

I just wanted to be recognized. I wanted to matter, as opposed to be-ing overshadowed or just pushed aside. I wanted people to know me. I wanted to be able to say "I'm here," and have people recognize the fact that I was somebody .

MICKEY: Getting into porn, how did that come about?

TANNER: I started when I turned 31, and when I consulted Chi Chi I was almost 32 years old. Chi Chi told it to me straight, she said, "Look, you are 10 years older than other people in this business. If you're going to do it, just do it and have a game plan."

MICKEY: Has the accident hurt you as far as how you're able to have sex?

TANNER: Since the accident, I had sex two times—I mean with people other than those in the porn industry—and we ended up jacking off each other. It's my arm. The way it looks I'm still sensitive about.

MICKEY: Were you right handed?

TANNER: I'm right handed, yes, so I learned how to write with my left now, and—

MICKEY: Oh, no, not that—

TANNER: Yes, I had to learn how to masturbate with my left hand. I'm getting better at it. I did a scene for All Worlds recently and they told me that I could still wear my arm brace if I wanted to. I can take it off but I have to hold it in certain positions, and bring lots of Ben Gay.

MICKEY: How did that go?

TANNER: These people can give a shit about my brace, they let me go at it and said, "Give us a Tanner Reeves scene," and that was nice. It was [director] Bill Hunter.

MICKEY: Were you aware of how many movies you've done?

TANNER: I don't own or see my movies, I don't now the names or what I'm in—that's kind of funny. Even though I don't own any of my movies I miss it and miss being in it. I fought really hard last year not to go into my shell again.

MICKEY: We're glad you didn't!

TANNER: I'm not going to shrivel up and die, I'm going to stay in it as long as people want me.

From **Chi Chi LaRue's Hardbody Video Magazine #1**

The Bare Facts

Birthday: January 3, 1962
Zodiac Sign: Capricorn
Chinese Zodiac: Tiger
Hair: Brown
Eyes: Gray-blue hazel
Height: 6-foot, 4-inches
Weight: 205 pounds
Cock Size: 9 inches
Favorite Color: Purple
Born: Detroit, Michigan
Resides: Santa Ana, Calif.
Workout Schedule: Two hours, three days a week.

Videography

6969 Melrose, *Bacchus Releasing*
All Man , *Hard as Steel/ Vivid Man Video*
At Your Service, *Academy Video/Planet Group*
Bedroom Lies, *Vivid Video*
Best of Daryl Brock, *Catalina Video*
Bi Conflict, *Forum Studios*
Big Drill, *Video 10*
Blowout, *Vivid Man*
Body of Art, *Thrust Studios*
Boot Black, *HIS Video Gold*
Boys From Bel Air, *Catalina Video*
Brief Exchanges, *HIS Video*
Captain Stud and his Seamen, *Sierra Pacific*
CD-Ram, *Men of Odyssey*
Centerspread 2, *Vivid Man Videos*
Chi Chi LaRue's Hardbody Video Magazine #1, *Men of Odyssey*
Clubhouse, *Totally Tight Video*
Come Closer, *Forum Studio*
Conflict of Interest, *Forum Studio*
Constant Hunger,

Close-Up Productions
Cruise Control, *Catalina*
Cybersex, *Bacchus Releasing*
Dildo Pigs, *Stallion*
Dirty White Guys, *All Worlds Video*
Dream Men, *Erotic Men/Midnight*
Drop 'Em, *Blade Productions/Video 10*
Dynastud 2, *HIS Video*
Eaten Alive, *Night Hawk Productions*
Friendly Desire, *Forum Studio*
Getting in Tight, *Forum Studio*
Hairy Chested Hunks, *Close-Up Productions*
Hand to Hand, *Vivid Man*
Hard Bodyguard, *HIS Video*
Hard Drive, *HIS Video Gold*
Hidden Instinct, *Catalina Video*
Hole Patrol, *Planet Group*
Horny & Hung, Vol. 12, *Leisure*
Hot Cops 2, *Centaur Films*
Hot Laguna Knights, *Iron Man/Metro*
Hot Stuff, *Video 10*
Hustling Roommate, *Butch Video/ Planet Group*
Idol Country, *HIS Video Gold*
Idol Inn Exile, *Catalina*
Illicit Love, *Metro Home Video*
In the Mix, *All Worlds Video*
In/Out Masseur, *Numbers Video*
Initiation 2, *Vivid Video*
Initiation, *Vivid Video*
Insiders, *Man's Best*
Intensive, *Metro Home Video*
Knight Gallery 2, *Vivid Man Video*
Leather Intrusion 3, *Video 10*
Leather Lover, *Sex Video/Video 10*
Leather Obsession 6: **The Search**, *Forum Studios*

Leather Virgin,
Leather Entertainment
Leatherworld,
Leather Entertainment
License to Thrill, *Sierra Pacific*
Long Play, *Video 10*
Lust Shack,
Blade Productions/Video 10
Male Order Sex, *Metro Home Video*
Man Construction, *HIS Video*
Man To Man, *Vivid Man Video*
Masculine Men, *Rebel Video/Leisure Time Entertainment*
Military Issue 2, *Forum Studios*
Military Issue 3, *Forum Studios*
Mind Blower, *Planet Group*
More Than Friends,
Karen Dior Productions
Moving Target, *Thrust Studios*
Navy Seals, *Totally Tight Video*
A Night With Todd Stevens,
Vivid Man Video
Nymphomania, *HIS Video*
Outcall Lover, *Bacchus Releasing*
Outlaw Bikers, *Triplex Productions*
Palm Springs Cruisin',
Video 10/Sex Video
Peep-O-Rama, *Catalina Video*
Phone Mates, *All Worlds Video*
Physical Education, *Video 10*
Pitch A Tent, *Catalina Video*
Playing Dirty, *Millennium Studios*
Politically Erect,
Big Bone Productions/Planet Group
Poolside Passions,
Azure Productions
Prisoner of Love, *Vivid Man*

Punk, *Vivid Man*
Pure Sex, *Bacchus Releasing*
Raw Stock, *HIS Video*
Receiving End, *Mustang*
Reflections of Sex, *Metro Home Video*
Remembering Times Gone Bi,
All Worlds Video
Roundup,
Academy Video/Planet Group
Santa Monica Place, *HIS Video*
Sex Posse, *Men of Odyssey*
Sexabition, *Image Video*
Sleeping Booty, *Sex Video*
Solicitor, *Vivid Man Video*
Stockade, *Metro Home Video*
Stud Valley, *Men of Odyssey*
Studs in Uniform, *Erotic Men*
Summer Daze, *HIS Video*
Summer Of Scott Randsome,
Catalina Video
Surrogate Stud,
Vizuns/Planet Group
Tight End, *Vidmax Video*
Too Big to Handle,
Jet Set Productions
Top Men,
Scorpion Entertainment/Video 10
Trade, *Malibu Sales*
Trickmaster,
Zack Video/Planet Group
Wear It Out, *Spectrum*
Wharfmen, *Russo Productions/Close Up Productions*
White Walls,
Inferno Blue Men/Sunshine

Adam Rom

"They usually tell you to not ejaculate a couple of days before the shoot, but I can't wait two days...You tell me to cum and I can cum in a moment's notice if I have a strong erection."

A dam Rom is one of the first exports that benefited the United States when the Iron Curtain came down. He is an iron-cocked, dependable guy with a heavy accent and an open quality which fans respond to in letters even since he's been in semi-retirement. He wants to work more behind-the-scenes and is working with former superstar Kevin Glover at Aries Post, an editing lab which does a lot of work for the adult industry.

I spent a weekend with gorgeous, Russian-born Adam in Chicago at the Man's Country bathhouse and—before you get any ideas—he was a total gentleman. Adam has a sleek, cut body and a stunning personality with an infectious smile and always, always accommodates fans. One of his biggest (and wealthiest) fans flew out from New York City just to see him perform at the bathhouse and Adam willingly spent a whole evening posing for pictures as well as signing autographs.

His favorite videos to date are **In Man's Country**, the Studio 2000 hit in which he seduces the just-coming-out Sonny Markham in a locker-room, **Point of View** from Studio 2000, and **Ultimate Reality** from Minotaur. He enjoys rollerblading in his spare time and swimming in the ocean, something he couldn't possibly do in Russia.

He's had a few bumps in his video career with not-so-good appearances in videos, but a few of his recent starring roles in big budget, big company videos are sure to catapult him to cult status. This interview comes in sections, as we talked on the jet to Chicago, in Leona's Italian restaurant while eating pasta with legendary director John Travis, and sitting in the bathhouse green room before he went on stage. The curly haired brunet has patience, and as you'll tell from the interview—we almost didn't make it to his dance gig!

Adam Rom

In **Personals**

At LAX Airport on our way to Chicago with a stopover in St. Louis. It was storming.

MICKEY: So, your first video was **Hard Labor** with my friend Jamie [director and former pornstar Jamie Hendrix]?

ADAM: Yes, I've always been curious to try that kind of business. He offered me the first opportunity and I tried it and I liked it.

MICKEY: Did you always know you were gay?

ADAM: I've been gay ever since I've been conscious of sexuality.

MICKEY: When did you get started?

ADAM: Only in May 1995. I found an ad from Jamie Hendrix and he took a look at me and said I would be good, but I thought I was a bit fat, so I got into shape to be acceptable.

MICKEY: Here's your horoscope: Aries. It says you are critical of yourself and traveling during this time is not good.

ADAM: Uh oh, John Travis is an Aries, too. We're both on this flight.

MICKEY: Two Aries, I'm surrounded by, maybe I shouldn't get on the plane with you two.

Sure enough, we missed our layover. While we were stuck in St. Louis, as director John Travis bought us margaritas, we continued the interview. We missed our plane because we were at the bar, drinking, but mostly smoking. Adam is a chain smoker.

MICKEY: So, you grew up in Russia?

ADAM: I grew up in Russia. I had the opportunity to come to the United States, but I didn't know but a little English. I was going to college to major in History and English to become a high school teacher. I had a year to go before I graduated. I never went back to school.

MICKEY: Does your family knows you're gay?

ADAM: Yes, I had no problem coming out.

MICKEY: Anything about the porn industry that surprised you?

ADAM: Yes, very much. The most healthy people I ever hung around are porn people. Hardly anyone drinks, and no one smokes as much as I do. People care what they eat, there's lots of vegetarians. Guys like J.T. Sloan taught me what to eat and what not to eat.

MICKEY: That's nice for you.

Waiting in first class for our plane to take off after missing our flight, and fearing we'd be stuck in St. Louis overnight, we decide to take a bit more of a breather. Adam isn't in a great mood, and sometimes we have to shout our triple-XXX conversation to each other. (He had an ear ache on the plane.)

MICKEY: Why did you get into the business? Most guys say it's for the money.

ADAM: For me it wasn't for the money; I needed to do it for self esteem.

MICKEY: Does it help?

ADAM: The people behind the scenes are like a family, they care about what happens to you personally. I worked a few times with Chi Chi LaRue who is very understanding and gives you time to do good work and makes you look good on camera. She gives a very, very energetic sense on the set.

Finally getting a connection, the rainstorm lets up and we're sent to the wrong airport in Chicago. Our bags were at yet another airport across town, and we're in a taxi heading into the city at last.

MICKEY: When you were growing up in Russia, were there other gay guys?

ADAM: There were so many people out, as in very out.

MICKEY: But you did fool around?

ADAM: Yes, I did, but it wasn't really talked about, it was just a sexual urge, and people tried lots of things.

MICKEY: When did that change?

ADAM: Well, I got a lesson from one man who taught me how to be affectionate and then I made friends who had boyfriends.

MICKEY: Did you ever have a relationship with a woman?

ADAM: Not really, but women do attract me. It's just that there're more men who make me hard than women.

MICKEY: So how do you identify sexually?

ADAM: I can't identify as gay, straight or bisexual because I really don't like those labels. I do say I'm gay, but I think that just serves as a political statement. Labels are terrible. They are used to make you something different or make you feel inferior.

MICKEY: Have you told friends back in Russia you do adult movies?

ADAM: Yes, they can get them now, and they do. Some of my friends just stumbled across me on a box. They don't perceive me as sexual, so to see me on a porn box was a shock. There was one friend who rented a video and saw a hot guy on the box and then saw me having sex with the guy and couldn't watch it anymore because he said it was like watching his sister have sex. He said he was shocked.

MICKEY: So you can get porn movies there?

ADAM: That's where I first saw a porno, with Jeff Stryker—**Powertool**.

MICKEY: Is he one of the guys you'd like to work with if you could?

ADAM: Oh yes, Jeff Stryker. He's someone I'd love to work with. He or Rex Chandler I'd like to work with. Everyone I like is either retired or impossible to get to work with.

MICKEY: Anyone else?

ADAM: Well yes, let me see: Steven Marks, but he quit, too, like Rex Chandler. Sometimes you think if you work with them it would spoil it because your imagination is better. I like a lot of kissing in my scenes and I like guys who kiss well. I don't think Stryker and Chandler kiss well, but I would like to train them.

We're more relaxed now, and we're talking while sitting at Leona's in the gay district of Chicago, waiting while fellow pornstar and Adam's co-star Sonny Markham gets a haircut.

MICKEY: Which guys have you enjoyed working with in videos?

ADAM: There was Chad Conners, he has a great ass.

MICKEY: And how was it with Sonny Markham?

ADAM: He is a great co-star in **In Man's Country**, because although he was straight for the most part, he has a sexual appeal that shows hesitation and uncertainty, and that is very appealing. It's almost innocent. It gave me lots of confidence. It made me want to do the best. We were both concerned about our performance. He is the favorite guy I've worked with so far.

At Berlin's disco standing at the bar, Adam and I share drinks and he has fans coming up to him. One asks him for an autograph and gushes over him. Adam blushed.

MICKEY: That guy who came up was so excited to meet you!

ADAM: I guess I'm getting used to the recognition—it was unnerving at first.

MICKEY: You gave him a big kiss; he'll never wash his cheek again.

ADAM: Sometimes I do that, if people are nice.

MICKEY: It seemed to make his day.

ADAM: Yeah, the way I handle fans is that if you're nice, and I think you want it, I'll plant a big wet kiss on you.

MICKEY: That's nice.

ADAM: I know that people are hesitant to come up and talk to me, so I make it easier for them. It helps build their self esteem—mine, too.

MICKEY: I can't believe that you have poor self esteem.

ADAM: I was insecure about my physical self when I first got into the sex business. When people do recognize me I used to get kind of shy.

MICKEY: But people think you're so cute!

ADAM: People say I'm good looking, but I don't think so, I have lots of wrinkles when I smile. I have to do that a bit more softly on video.

MICKEY: But it's such a cute smile!

ADAM: Thanks. Maybe you can't see so in this dark club, but I'm blushing.

At Man's Countrys bathhouse in the green room upstairs above the stage, Adam's about to go out and dance among his fans and will soon be totally naked. But for now, he's wearing jeans, sneakers and a T-shirt. He is a bit nervous as we survey the men in towels from above and see them sitting in anticipation around the stage, waiting for the main act—Adam Rom.

MICKEY: You certainly have a lot of fans. That guy came all the way from New York to see you.

ADAM: It's really nice to see how many people recognize your work, I'm always flattered. That guy knew every title I ever did, and he could name the people I did scenes with. He knew my résumé better than I did.

MICKEY: You handle it well.

ADAM: It's almost like I have to develop a different type of personality for Adam.

MICKEY: Like how?

ADAM: He's nasty, more physical, more an exhibitionist.

MICKEY: Does that work?

ADAM: They think I'm very expensive. (*Laughs*)

Just after his dance number, Adam is sitting in only a towel back up in the green room. The numbers he did were hot. He got a standing ovation out there, and some of the guys had a standing ovation in their towels, too!

MICKEY: The guy you pulled from the audience during your dance number seemed quite amused.

ADAM: And aroused. I like to do that. I try to find someone who isn't that nervous. This was my first big dance audience that I performed in front of, so I was nervous. I loved the people. As soon as the applause came, it was OK.

MICKEY: So this was your first experience in a club like this?

ADAM: Yes, it makes me more confident about going on the dance circuit.

During a driving tour of the city the next day, Adam and I get a bit more personal.

MICKEY: Do your parents know what you do?

ADAM: No, but they are very liberal. However, we never talked about sex at all around the house, that was a no-no subject.

MICKEY: What was it like growing up in Russia? Was it difficult to be gay there? Did you have to fake being heterosexual?

ADAM: I went out with girls in school, but I had had my first experience with guys by then.

MICKEY: Really? At an early age, then? Did you feel any stigma attached to your attraction to men? Is that something you grew up with in the former Soviet Union?

ADAM: Yes, I just thought it was something that was wrong with me that I would grow out of.

Late at night at his hotel room where Adam was trying on new outfits for his second show the next day, we continued more of a private chat. He was stripping in front of me and I was trying to keep eye contact as he peeled off his tight Spandex and leather outfits; his huge cock was semi-erect as he tried to stuff it inside his briefs.

MICKEY: What kind of guy are you attracted to?

ADAM: What I look for is someone who has imagination. Someone who has nice eyes, legs and face.

MICKEY: Any particular age?

ADAM: Usually I like someone younger or the same age.

MICKEY: Any particular look you like better?

ADAM: It doesn't have to be someone super attractive, but I like the person's eyes. It doesn't matter what they have in their pants, but it does in their face.

MICKEY: And how fast do you sleep with someone?

ADAM: I have a strict rule that I don't change. I never sleep with the guy right away. Not until the third date. That freaks some guys out, I know, but I insist on that. People think it's odd for me because I get paid to have sex with someone on sets even though I first meet them right there, but it's not the same in someone's personal life.

*At the Leather Museum in Chicago where we were touring the nasty exhibits with Ron Ehman. And then dinner with Ron and Chuck Renslow, the **Man's Country** owner, and his wonderful "family" of friends. The "family" is very taken with Adam, and ask him a lot of questions.*

MICKEY: Why do you do this?

ADAM: I have a good answer to that. I saw Jim Carrey on Oscar night a few years ago and he said his father was an accountant and lost his job and almost had to move his family into the streets. There is no secure job now, so I figure why not? You might as well do what you like to do rather than stick to a job you hate because it's supposedly secure.

At breakfast the next morning, I click on the tape recorder and continue my in-depth probe. (I ate his sausage—from his plate!)

MICKEY: How long do you see your career going?

ADAM: I am planning on being a model for a couple more years. My agent is Johnny Johnston and he says he thinks I have a few more years left in me.

MICKEY: Do you want to do something else in the industry?

Photo courtesy: Studio 2000

Photo courtesy: Studio 2000

Photo courtesy: Mickey Skee

(Top) In the popular Chicago bathhouse filming **In Man's Country**, (Bottom) touring the Leather Museum.

ADAM: Yes, I enjoy editing and other things. I can see myself directing someday. Director Ross Cannon has shown me the ropes behind the scenes, and I'm learning from him as well as Kevin Glover.

MICKEY: So you think you can direct?

ADAM: Like anything else, I'd like to give it a try.

*On the way home, while watching **Golden Eye** on the jet back, we get a bit bored and talk some more.*

MICKEY: You seem very accommodating to your fans.

ADAM: Of course, and all the porn boys should do the same.

MICKEY: They don't all do that?

ADAM: No, some of them treat their fans like shit. I know, I've seen it—but if someone is coming to see you perform, you give it your best. You don't want them to be disappointed.

MICKEY: I love your charming accent.

ADAM: Oh that! I could get rid of that accent in two months if I really tried. Some voice coach once told me that they can work with me to get rid of my accent, but I don't want to, it's part of my charm and I don't want to lose it.

MICKEY: Is there anything you want to say to your fans out there?

ADAM: I want to thank you all for admiring me. Write me through my friend Mickey Skee, and I'll write back, I promise.

The Bare Facts

Birthday: April 17, 1970
Zodiac Sign: Aries
Chinese Zodiac: Dog
Hair: Brown
Eyes: Deep brown
Height: 5-foot, 10-inches
Weight: 155 pounds
Cock Size: 8 inches
Favorite Color: Red
Born: Western Russia
Resides: Hollywood, Calif.
Workout Schedule: One hour, three times a week.

Videography

976-HOTT, Part 2, *Midnight Men*
After Hours, *Vivid Man Video*
Alley Boys, *Catalina*
Alibi For A Gang Bang, *BIG Video*
Blow Hard, *Catalina*
Born to Please, *Video 10*
Boys Behind Bars #4,
  Midnight Men
Boys from Berlin,
  Jamie Hendrix Productions
Boys of Big Sur,
  Pleasure Productions
Bustin' Loose, *Centaur Films*
The Choice,*Huge Video*
Cram Course: Sex Ed #3, *Minotaur*
Cum-Bustible, *All Worlds Video*
Daddy's Dudes, *Stallion*
Fireside Brats, *YMAC Videos*
Gang Bang Belgium Boy,
  BIG Video

Gino Colbert's Hunk Hunt 7,
  Super Stallion
Guys Like Us, *Hot House*
Hard Ass, *Leisure Time*
Hard Labor, *Spectrum Video*
Hot Cops 3, *Centaur Films*
Hot Male Mechanics,
  Bacchus Releasing
Hunk Hunt #4,
  Leisure Time Entertainment
In Man's Country, *Studio 2000*
Masculine Men, *Rebel Video*
Oral Alley, *Catalina*
Personals, *Vivid Man*
Playing Hard, *Midnight Men*
Pleasure Ridge, *Spectrum Video*
Point of View, *Studio 2000*
Rescue 69-11, *Vivid Man Video*
Rocket Ryder, *All Worlds Video*
Showboys,
  Showboys Entertainment
Studio Tricks, *Catalina*
Taking the Plunge,
  Man Splash Video
Tight Places, *Midnight Men*
Top Men, *Scorpion Entertainment*
Ultimate Reality, *Minotaur*
Uncut Weekend, *Oh Man! Studios*

Marco Rossi

"You see, I like sex. I have no problem with any kind of sex. I like getting off, I like other people getting off, I especially like other people getting off watching me."

There was a time when Marco Rossi spurned my drunken advances at a bar. Then, there was the time he shot a big load all over my kitchen counter. Now before you get any ideas nastier than I've already laid out, both of those were for videos. The first was in Forum Studio's **Romeo & Julian**, in which I had a non-speaking cameo—I played a bar troll, and I yanked a dollar out of Marco's crotch while he was dancing on the bar. (The best part was cut by director Sam Abdul, but he tells me everybody says that.) And the cumshot in my kitchen was for a scene in **The Bartender.**

I spied Marco Rossi during filming in a Beverly Hills mansion for HIS Video's **Idol Country**, with Ryan Idol. I also noticed him when he made the special collector's issue of *Men's Workout* magazine, in 1994. Even today, Marco enters body building competitions with Tom Katt.

I've sat with Marco on Chi Chi LaRue's bed watching his latest work fresh from the editing room. I've danced with him in Las Vegas at a gay club, walked West Hollywood streets with him during Halloween and hung out with his friendly, pornstar girlfriend at nightclubs along with starlet Sharon Kane.

When he was shooting **The Bartender** at my house in the Hollywood Hills, as he stood on my back porch totally naked, we did some of this interview. He first dried his hair with my blow dryer and then sat out on the breakfast porch with me while director Sam Abdul shot another scene with two hard hunks just a few feet away.

We talked about his rumored team-up with Ryan Idol, his hot desert photo spread with a horse and the beer bottle trick which led to the infamous Club 404 Austin incident in which he got busted by undercover cops.

In **The Look of A Man**

He's always been known as a superbrat! But, he's less of a brat these days; he's really sweet, actually, despite the rough Queens accent that he'll never be able to hide. He has a flawless body, a cute, dimpled cheek and a super personality. I've dubbed him the new Italian Stallion, and he is.

Get ready to see a new-and-improved Marco Rossi. He wants to do more beefy roles, even though he's been around for awhile and now is considered one of the grand-daddies of gay video (or at least a veteran). He thinks he's earned a good role written just for him, something he can act in, something he can really sink his teeth into. He smiles when he says that.

MICKEY: You've always seemed to enjoy the roles you really get to act a lot in.

MARCO: You know what it's like, Mickey—most porn videos don't have good acting. So when I get one of those rare roles, I have a lot of fun with them.

MICKEY: Are directors still pressuring you to do a bottom scene?

MARCO: Yeah, yeah. I should be more versatile, perhaps, in the sexual positions that I do, but I want good acting roles, too.

MICKEY: Tell me how you got started in this—you have a degree in college, don't you?

MARCO: I worked right after high school in this dead-end job. I worked at brokerage firms wearing a suit, getting up and doing the commuting thing at five o'clock in the morning. This was the furthest thing from my mind. I was studying physical therapy and liberal arts, in college, but I didn't get a degree. I may go back to that someday.

MICKEY: You took some time off and now you're back in videos again with **The Bartender**?

MARCO: That's right, it was a conscious choice. After a long dry spell, I finally get a role that I can sink my teeth and cock into.

MICKEY: Sounds like a great role: how come you're not getting more stuff like this?

MARCO: Maybe I'm not getting the roles anymore because I've got that brat reputation. I admit I'm a spoiled brat.

MICKEY: Do you still love to watch your videos?

MARCO: I love to watch my videos.

MICKEY: Do you consider yourself gay or straight?

MARCO: I guess I'm 70 percent straight and 30 percent gay but there's that side of me that gets off watching gay porn.

MICKEY: I hear you're taking acting classes?

MARCO: Acting, you either have it or you don't. I want a good role someday, to have something written for me, so I'm putting the word out.

MICKEY: I watched you on the set of **Idol Country**; you did good there and that part was written for you.

MARCO: That was a time when I did a really good job with Grant Larson, but it could've been better. I was shaking, I was nervous. I want a bigger script than that, though. Some companies won't hire me now even though I'm better built than ever before.

MICKEY: Why is that?

MARCO: They're waiting for me to bottom. Chi Chi LaRue said that if I were more versatile on screen then I'd be back up there—not that I think I came down that far. You would know better than me.

MICKEY: To be on top you have to be a bottom nowadays?

MARCO: Right. Chi Chi offered me two movies if I did, but I don't want to resort to that just yet.

MICKEY: Whatever happened to the project Ryan Idol was telling me about with your topping him? Now that could help both your careers. That would be hot.

MARCO: I don't know why that never happened. He wanted to top me, then it was the other way. It would have been a good contrast, the two of us.

MICKEY: You know that could change in a moment.

MARCO: I wanted it to happen in **Idol Country**, even an oral scene with him, but I don't want to do a movie with me worshipping him. I want to be a star, too.

MICKEY: So will we see Marco Rossi bottoming soon?

MARCO: By next year—yeah, probably. I'm in really, really good shape, maybe I'll do it.

MICKEY: Who would you do it with?

MARCO: Ryan Idol would have done it, I loved Scott Baldwin, but that won't happen now either. I was supposed to do something with Windsor Group, but that company fell through. I don't know. Everyone says they want me to bottom, over and over. I don't know what's the big deal about this bottom thing.

MICKEY: Speaking of bottom, you have a handy trick with your bottom and a beer bottle. Tell us about the Club 404 Austin incident.

MARCO: Oh, yeah, that was wild. We were to perform at a club. I was there with Chi Chi LaRue. The owner was really nice and holding a private party. He told us "you can do your own show after 12:30," it was definitely entrapment.

MICKEY: There were police undercover in the audience?

MARCO: Yeah, they shut the doors to the club and didn't let anyone

Photo courtesy: Odyssey Men Video

Photo courtesy: Forum

Photo courtesy: Mustang Studios

Photo courtesy: Vivid Man

Clockwise from top left: **Chi Chi La Rue's Hard Body #3**, **Leather Obsession 2**, **Marco Rossi—A Wanted Man**, and **Double Vision**.

else in and they let us do this really nasty show. We were on a 26-city tour throughout the country and did the same thing in other cities, mostly for private shows. Derek Cruise was allowed to dance with only his cap in front of his crotch and I could do the bottle trick.

MICKEY: Which is?

MARCO: I essentially take the neck of a beer bottle up my butt.

MICKEY: So you did the show uninterrupted, the cops enjoyed it, and then what happened?

MARCO: They came backstage and arrested me. Chi Chi followed me to the jail and my agent at the time, David Forest, bailed me out.

MICKEY: There was such a public outcry, too!

MARCO: Yeah, they made T-shirts about it and sell the shirts in Texas to pay for my legal bills.

MICKEY: Do you have a favorite director?

MARCO: Chi Chi, of course; she is the one who got me started.

MICKEY: How did you get your start? Wasn't it through that handsome one-named pornstar, Damian, who is also now retired?

MARCO: It was in Palm Springs through Damian, who introduced me to Chi Chi. But before Chi Chi, I met other people in the business. I first met John Travis from Studio 2000 at Webster Hall, in Manhattan, where Jeff Stryker was performing. I was go-go dancing and he suggested I come out to California. Then I met Damian, and Chi Chi brought me out for **Mirage**. LaRue was great, she took it easy on me in an oral scene and it was real simple.

MICKEY: Was that difficult at all?

MARCO: Not at all—see, I like sex, and sex is sex, if it's a guy or girl.

MICKEY: Do you identify as bisexual?

MARCO: I don't define myself as fully straight; I guess I'd have bisexual tendencies. There's a type who I prefer to have. If I work with a guy, I might not be attracted to him, but we just have sex.

MICKEY: What is the kind of guy you like to have sex with?

MARCO: I like dark haired Italians, someone like myself, but much older.

MICKEY: Do you like it rough?

MARCO: More passionate than rough. I like kissing. I like sex and being sensual. I like it rough sometimes, but not pulling hair or anything like that. (*Laughs*)

MICKEY: What do you like in women?

MARCO: I like a woman who is a gay guy in a woman's body. A woman with masculine energy.

MICKEY: You want to do mainstream acting roles someday, too?

MARCO: I do want to do more acting on television—on **Melrose Place**, or, I'd be good in a **Beverly Hills, 90210** role.

MICKEY: Do you think porn will hurt you?

MARCO: Not any more these days. Anything can affect me. I'm not going to put it behind me, I won't deny it. But I won't come out with it.

MICKEY: What about all the fans bugging you? I hear and see them all the time all over you when we're out together at a club or something.

MARCO: Sure—I don't mind it, though. I have a fan club of 150 members—it's more than Ryan Idol has—and they write me all kinds of kinky letters. I haven't even read them all. It's nice. Fans during my shows tell me different things, like how to dance, and I should do this or that. That's something I take to heart. People are totally into my body, and that is nice.

MICKEY: I met your girlfriend, Lana Sands, in Las Vegas and really like her. Where did you first meet her?

MARCO: I met Lana Sands at the Night of the Stars. Chi Chi introduced me, and since August 1994 we've been together. We must get along because we're in the same business.

MICKEY: She doesn't mind you fucking guys?

MARCO: She does too, and girls. We know it's work, and we're always safe.

MICKEY: Have you done straight videos?

MARCO: There is one out there with Lana and I, it's called **Lana Exposed**, by V-Team Video.

MICKEY: Could you ever have a boyfriend?

MARCO: I can't have a boyfriend because I know how guys are out there—they're not faithful when they have a relationship with a guy, and I want someone who can be faithful to me.

MICKEY: That's tough to find all right.

MARCO: Tell me about it. I want a pal, a buddy, not more of the same old sex, but a pal. It's hard to find.

The Bare Facts

Birthday: October 16, 1970
Zodiac Sign: Libra
Chinese Zodiac: Dog
Hair: Black
Eyes: Walnut brown
Height: 5-foot, 10-inches
Weight: 180 pounds
Cock Size: 7 inches
Favorite Color: Black
Born: Queens, New York
Resides: Laguna, Calif.
Workout Schedule: Twice a day, five times a week.

Videography

Ace in the Hole, *Catalina Videos*
Back Room, *Falcon Studios*
The Bartender, *Forum Studios*
Best of Sam Abdul, *Forum Studios*
Chi Chi LaRue's Hard Body 3,
   Men of Odyssey
Day of Decadence,
   Vivid Man Video
Double Vision, *Mustang Studios*
Dripping Hard 3, *Rage Collection*
Driven To It, *Studio 2000*
Fame & Flesh, *HIS Video Gold*
The Getaway, *Catalina Videos*
Grease Guns, *Studio 2000*
Hands On, *Mustang Studios*

House Rules, *Falcon Studios*
How to Get a Man in Bed,
   Forum Studios
Idol Country, *HIS Video Gold*
International Male Leather
   Uncut, *Catalina Video*
Knight Gallery, *Vivid Man*
Lana Exposed, *V-Team Video*
Latex Meltdown, *Can-Am/Masta*
Leather Obsession 2,
   Forum Studios
License to Thrill, *Fox Studios*
Long Play, *Triple X*
The Look of A Man,
   Mustang Studios
Man's Touch, *HIS Interactive CD*
Marco Rossi—A Wanted Man,
   Vivid Man
Masquerade, *Men of Odyssey*
Mess Hall Maneuvers, *Tyger Films*
Military Issue, *Forum Studios*
Mirage, *Jocks Studios*
Night Fall, *Paladin*
Night Heat, *Paladin*
Romeo & Julian, *Forum Studios*
Stripper Service, *HIS Video Gold*
Stroking It, Uncut, *Junior Studios*
Total Corruption, *HIS Video Gold*
The Urge, *Vivid Man*
Virtual Viewer Photodisc,
   HIS Interactive CD
A Wanted Man, *Vivid Video*

Derrick
Stanton

"Normally, I have to put myself into my own fantasy to keep it hard, but now that I'm back after more than a decade and I'm working with some of the guys these days, I have no problem—they're really sexy."

The first time I met the legendary Derrick Stanton, I was speechless. He appeared on the set of Jerry Douglas' **Flesh & Blood** with short-cropped, silvery hair and his beautiful Asian lover of seven years, Quan, a guy who looks stunning in drag, and a big fan of porn. It was hard to believe that Stanton, this classic Bill Higgins model, still looked as sexy as ever. It was even harder to realize that being on the set with him that day—while watching masterful director Jerry Douglas work out a complicated six-man orgy scene—marked the beginnings of Stanton's return to the business. What cinched it for him was seeing how oddly professional the whole business had become; he was itching to give it another go.

He watched the sets, thought about it, discussed it with his lover, and finally agreed to make a comeback—almost two decades after he started doing videos.

Of course, I jumped at the chance to see him in person and naked on the set of Chi Chi LaRue's **Hard Core** video shoot in North Hollywood for All Worlds Video. I walked into the dressing room and he stood there fully nude with his cock semi-erect, and it was nice to see that the 41-year-old legend still had it all. He took off the black mask he was wearing, slipped on some jeans and sat to talk while chomping on a huge Subway sandwich in director T.J. Paris' office. I sat at the desk. Derrick stretched out on a red vinyl sofa in front of me.

MICKEY: I'm so honored that you're going to be part of this book.

DERRICK: I'm honored to be part of it. I'm flattered. I'm also surprised that I'm not the oldest guy in it.

In **Family Values**

MICKEY: True, I think Cole Tucker beats you out by a few years.

DERRICK: I never thought that I would be thought of so highly in the industry—being in a book and getting these Hall of Fame awards.

MICKEY: Guys are interested in you, and they're interested in guys your age being in videos right now.

DERRICK: It seems to be mirroring some of the trends of what people say they are interested in. I was interested in older guys when I was younger. Now, my lover is 13 years younger than me.

MICKEY: This is the second Hall of Fame award for you. The first one was for the *Gay Video Guide* awards, and this one recently is for the *Adult Video News* Hall of Fame, which is like the Oscars of porn.

DERRICK: I was very surprised that it was given to me. I mean, there're so many others to recognize, such as Kip Noll or Steve York. It's an honor.

MICKEY: Well deserved, too. Are people beginning to recognize you again now that you're back doing videos?

DERRICK: It was funny, I picked up a copy of *Nightlife* and there I was on the cover with a **Family Values** photo and it wasn't a bad picture. I almost didn't recognize it at first.

MICKEY: You worked with the only pornstar I've ever had a relationship with, the late Johnny Dawes in **Bad Bad Boys**. What was that like?

DERRICK: Johnny was a real nice kid; I didn't know you knew him. We always had a lot of fun together. There was a photographer who once took a photo spread of Johnny and me and didn't pay us for it [the photographer is also long gone], and a theater owner at an adult theater told the guy, who was trying to promote one of his own videos, that he would have to pay the both of us right then and there before he left the theater or none of his movies would ever be shown there again. So, he went scrambling for the money and paid us.

MICKEY: When I met you on the **Flesh and Blood** set, was Jerry Douglas really priming you to do a scene then?

DERRICK: I was supposed to do a scene in **Flesh and Blood,** but something came up and I couldn't do it, and Jerry was angry about it, but he did invite me to come down and watch.

MICKEY: Has your going back into adult video affected your mainstream career at all?

DERRICK: No. I once had a guy at a house I was managing get mad at me and threaten to tell everyone at work I did porn, and I said, "Go ahead, no one would care." I don't think they would anymore.

MICKEY: What was it that first drew you to porn?

DERRICK: I think I was always a bit of an exhibitionist, even when I was a teenager; I would jack off outdoors and have sex where others may see me. I also went to bath houses a lot and loved it when guys got off watching me.

MICKEY: Tell me about the scene you play in this video.

DERRICK: In my scene [for **Hard Core**] I play Adam Hart's biggest fan and so [to prepare] for today I actually watched his videos last night and checked them all out before the scene today.

MICKEY: Really?

DERRICK: Yeah, and I thought Adam Hart's work was awesome; it really got me hard. It's great to see someone who looks real good who really puts a lot of feeling into it and tries to do his best job.

MICKEY: He's such a nice guy, too.

DERRICK: Wonderful. I wish all the straight or bisexual guys I worked with way back were like that, too. Adam Hart's truly charming. There was this guy Adam Mitchell I worked with way back in one of my first films—he said he was straight, but I think he was bisexual. He loved dick too much. We had an instant rapport, a good connection. Adam Hart reminds me a bit of him.

MICKEY: Did you get a chance to spend time with Adam Hart before you did a scene?

DERRICK: Yeah, some. We were talking earlier about some of the different people we've seen in this gay adult business who have attitude, and just feel like they have to stand there and do nothing just 'cause they're good looking, and they're really nothing.

MICKEY: That's not Adam, but there are a few guys who are still in the gay industry now who are that way.

DERRICK: I can tell that Adam really puts his heart and soul into it. Even in the stuff he directs.

MICKEY: Some people have so much attitude that it makes it tough for co-stars to get it up.

DERRICK: Yeah, it was always like that, even way back in my day.

MICKEY: Anything specific that was particularly difficult for you back in the old days?

DERRICK: One specific situation I can remember from back then was how guys were very strict about being a top or a bottom.

MICKEY: Even if they were gay?

DERRICK: Especially if they were gay. Some guys insisted they were never a bottom and it didn't even matter if they're gay or straight. Sometimes, though, these guys were the ones who couldn't get it up—you're waiting to be a bottom but they can't get it up at all.

MICKEY: Nowadays, it's mostly the straight guys who do that, the ones who get in the business and are gay-for-pay, but don't do anything except get serviced.

DERRICK: It's not a good thing. It wasn't back then, it isn't now.

MICKEY: What would happen back then, do you remember a specific incident?

DERRICK: Yeah, a guy who was an "only top" guy couldn't get it up. Then the director, in this case William Higgins, finally gets frustrated and says, "OK, unless you get it up in five minutes you're going to be the bottom if you want to get paid."

MICKEY: So what happened?

DERRICK: He didn't get it up and he had to be the bottom for me. He tightened his muscles, practically crossed his legs, and fought me every inch of the way, but he got fucked. I finally managed to make penetration. But that was an example of an extreme attitude.

MICKEY: What significant changes have you seen in porn videos from what it was like back then?

DERRICK: The music numbers that they put in some of these videos are great. I remember **Hart Attack**, that Adam Hart did, the music was outstanding in that. And the song that Sharon Kane did in **Family Values**, which was nominated in many awards shows. It was really good.

MICKEY: They never did original songs?

DERRICK: Back in my day, the music was almost always bouncing disco music and it didn't always fit. They put a bit more effort into it now.

MICKEY: One question I've always wanted to ask you is that it seemed, back then, that porn was a bit more legitimate, real, raw, hard-core sex, where guys just go at it, and now it's like there's a lot more orchestrated sex, pre-planned sex and simulated sex—is that right?

DERRICK: Yeah, they kind of just threw you in there. It was some-times just improvised and they said, "Do whatever you want to do" and that meant whatever sex act you felt like.

MICKEY: They even did that in the orgy scenes?

DERRICK: Yeah. Sometimes they put five or six guys together in a room and said "find a guy who you can get along with and go at it."

MICKEY: What about that classic orgy scene in **Class Reunion**?

DERRICK: In extreme cases, like **Class Reunion**, they took about 30 guys and put them in an outside swimming area and said "OK, pair off," and there was a group orgy and the camera just went around and took video.

MICKEY: Gosh, really?

DERRICK: It's changed a lot. What I've seen now, the crews seem a lot more professional. There's a lot more effort that goes into the production values.

MICKEY: The look of the guys seem different, too.

DERRICK: The guys are in much better physical condition. In the '70s and early '80s it was a lot more difficult to find guys who would do it as opposed to now.

MICKEY: Why is that?

DERRICK: Oh, the fear of retribution and being busted, that sort of thing, you don't see that as often because it's legit now.

MICKEY: You must have seen a big change in the way things are done now from how they were back then.

DERRICK: I've seen a big change. In 1997, when I started doing videos again, it had been 21 years since I'd done my first film. At age 41 I was pretty nervous doing a scene again. It worked out OK.

MICKEY: What's new to the business that surprises you?

DERRICK: It seems a lot of the stars today have an agent. That's a new phenomenon, I never saw the need for one. It's been helpful for some of the guys, so they tell me.

MICKEY: You quit the business because of a lover?

DERRICK: I quit in 1985 because my boyfriend at the time said, "Enough, this is the last one."

MICKEY: Did you miss it right away?

DERRICK: It took a few films before I actually did quit. I finally did.

At this point Chi Chi LaRue and Jordan Young (pornstar, script writer and production assistant) enter the room and Chi Chi asks Derrick: "You know what, if I need you would you just put your cock in a window? I need an indiscriminate cock in a window and since you can get hard in two seconds—" Derrick responds: "Well, at 41 it may take four seconds. Sure, I'll do it. That's simple enough. You owe me a nice dinner later."

MICKEY: How do you prepare to do a sex scene?

DERRICK: Normally, I have to put myself into my own fantasy to keep it hard, but now that I'm back after more than a decade and I'm working with some of the guys these days, I have no problem—they're really sexy. But, you have to have your own fantasies. It's because you're not always interested in the person you're with sometimes.

MICKEY: How is it having a relationship with someone who's not in the porn industry? Are there jealousies already developing?

DERRICK: Oh sure, a small bit. A lot of guys in gay relationships say, "Oh, we're open, you can do anything as long as I don't know about it," but then if they see you with someone there's this emotion that overwhelms them. Sometimes gay couples try to emulate straight couples and

Photo courtesy: Men Of Odyssey

Photo courtesy: Catalina Video

(Top) With Kurt Young in **Family Values**, (Bottom) in **Class of '84**

it's not always right, but it's how they were brought up.

MICKEY: You always seemed to be totally gay identified; have you had sex with women?

DERRICK: Well, let me tell you about myself; my initial experiences were with women. I've had sex with women and I've really enjoyed it. A pussy feels really good around a dick. I know that experience.

MICKEY: That's a controversial statement from the gay legend Derrick Stanton!

DERRICK: It reminds me of a good joke, "How do you know you've had a good night? When you wake up in the morning and your face feels like a glazed donut."

MICKEY: That's a pussy joke?

DERRICK: To me it was a turn-on to go down on a woman. In the '70s I used to have a mustache and that was the thing. The feeling of a woman cumming was exciting, it turned me on. But in my heart I knew I really enjoyed men.

MICKEY: Could you do it with a woman again?

DERRICK: Sure, I could; if the situation was right, I could have sex with a woman again. I consider myself gay because I go after men even if a woman comes up to me.

MICKEY: What about your family, do they know about your porn past by now? Or even that you're gay?

DERRICK: The way it was with my family, I figured that when they were ready to ask me if I was gay then I would tell them. The first thing my father did on Father's Day was ask me "Are you gay?" and I said, "Yes," and then he asked the next question and said, "Do you do porn?" I was aghast. My sister had a big mouth.

MICKEY: Your sister squealed on you?

DERRICK: Yeah, and my dad was very curious. He said, "Is it good? I'd like to see some."

MICKEY: Oh, my god—what did you say?

DERRICK: I said, "Dad, I don't think you should, I don't think you'd like it or understand it. My advice is that you not watch this."

MICKEY: Was he disappointed?

DERRICK: He had this image of me carrying on the family name. Seeing this—it would be a bit too shocking.

MICKEY: And did your friends ever see any of it, I mean friends you didn't have in the business, old school pals?

DERRICK: Yeah, I took some straight friends who wanted to see me in the films to the Century Theater, before it burned down, and the first thing we saw there was the movie where the guys are giving each other an enema and shooting it out and into each other's mouths, back and forth for about 15 minutes. These are people who never knew anything about gay sex. I said, "That's not what most people do in gay sex."

MICKEY: Did you watch yourself in videos, I mean recent ones?

DERRICK: I was nervous seeing **Family Values**, but they asked me to do it. When I saw the scene with Steve York, I realized there was a certain trashiness that's kind of hot—sex between an older and younger guy.

The Bare Facts

Birthday: October 27, 1955
Zodiac Sign: Scorpio
Chinese Zodiac: Sheep
Hair: Brown with a bit of gray showing
Eyes: Brown
Height: 6-feet
Weight: 175 pounds
Cock Size: 8 1/2-inches
Favorite Color: Green
Born: Baltimore, MD.
Resides: Huntington Beach, Calif.
Workout Schedule: Three times a week, an hour and half each time.

Videography

Bad Bad Boys, *Hand-in-Hand*
Best Of Kip Noll,
 William Higgins Video
Boys of Venice, *William Higgins Video*
Brothers Should Do It,
 Laguna *Pacific*
Class of '84, Part 1,
 William Higgins Video
Class of '84, Part 2,
 William Higgins Video
Class Reunion, *Catalina Video*
Family Values, *Men of Odyssey*
Grease Monkeys,
 William Higgins Video
Hard Core, *All Worlds Video*
Hardhat, *Jaguar Films*
The Idol, *Hand-in-Hand*
Jocks, *Hand-in-Hand*

Kip Noll: Superstar,
 William Higgins Video
L.A. Tool and Die, *HIS Video*
Members Only,
 William Higgins Video
Men Under The Hardhat,
 William Higgins Video
Performance, *Hand-in-Hand*
Printer's Devils,
 William Higgins Video
Rear Deliveries,
 William Higgins Video
Route 69, *William Higgins Video*
Strange Places and
 Strange Things,
 William Higgins Video
These Bases Are Loaded,
 Catalina Video
Tricking, *Nova Fortuna*
Wet Shorts, *William Higgins Video*

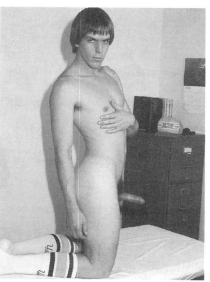

In **Class of '84**

Cole Tucker

"I am a versatile actor and I am versatile in real life, and I realize the best way for me to represent my sexuality is to be true to myself and be honest on film. I don't have this bottom/top thing."

He's as close to a live Popeye the Sailor Man as anyone could ever meet. Cole Tucker is strong to the finish, but he's also kind, just like his cartoon counterpart. He's in this book because not only is he one of the hottest newcomers in the porn business, he is the oldest gay pornstar who ever started the business (in his mid-40s), and he is riding the wave of recent surveys which all say that fans want to see older, rougher-looking guys like him.

We sat down at a restaurant only a day after I was on the set watching this massive-armed, tattooed, cigar-chomping hunk stand out dominantly in a "back alley" orgy with a dozen other men in Men of Odyssey's **Family Values**, the classic directed by Jerry Douglas. In person, this nasty, leather-clad star of **Acres of Ass, Catalinaville, Leather Obsession 6** and **Fallen Angel** is every bit as intimidating as on video—at first, that is.

Heads turned when he walked in at the French Market restaurant, in the heart of West Hollywood, for this interview. From young We-Ho pretty-boys to graying, nattily-dressed daddies they all wanted to look, to sniff. Cole Tucker not only talked about his age, his day job in real estate and his relationships, he actually teared up and cried during the interview when discussing how wonderfully he's been treated by people in the adult business this past year. He cried!

Not only is this guy a stud, he's sensitive, and he's exactly what the public wants—and perhaps what we all want—in a man.

MICKEY: What pre-conceived ideas did you have about the business that were totally wrong?

COLE: Everything. The whole business is completely different than

Cole Tucker

In **Catalinaville**

Photo courtesy: Catalina Video

before I got into it.

MICKEY: What did you think is was going to be?

COLE: First of all, I thought is was going to be easy. I thought it was going to be someone saying, "Oh, why don't you have sex with him and we'll get it on tape."

I didn't really have any pre-conceived notions that it was non-professional, yet the level of professionalism in this business surprised me.

MICKEY: What would you tell people about getting into the business?

COLE: If you're thinking of getting into this business, you need to do your homework and realize that these are professional people and this is a business. It is about money. It's about being on time. It's about delivering a product. It's about being pleasant and knowledgeable. It's about listening and giving and being kind. Those are the keys to being successful in this business.

MICKEY: Not just a big dick, eh?

COLE: Absolutely not. If you think you have to have the biggest dick, the greatest body, the prettiest face, some element in you that makes you sexually attractive—and everybody has that something—you're right. But to be successful, it appears to me you have to have more than that. You have to fit within the professional guidelines of this business and be easy to work with. And to help, not take away from the set. And I think on, movie number three I figured that all out. You know something, it is so easy to be nice. It's so easy.

MICKEY: It's refreshing to hear that. I know you are a fully 100 percent all-male homosexual. Have you had an issue with the gay-for-pay guys? You know, the ones who claim that they're straight and still take it up the butt?

COLE: I don't personally have an issue with them, but being in this business I kind of poll my friends about what they think and what they like to see. And it's coming back from my friends, the regular people that buy this stuff, the people we're doing this for, that people are tired of the straight guys in porn. I don't know why the three biggies all are straight-identified—is it a coincidence? Is it something you guys in the industry created as a mystique?

MICKEY: I don't know. I think it's changing. It's going to change.

COLE: I'm a gay man and I'm proud of it. I want to do a good job in this industry. I am a little different though. I don't have the traits or qualities to be at that highest level because you need to be generically appealing. And I have an edge to me which would rule out some markets. So, I don't expect that that could ever happen to me. I am just interested in getting to my fans. I think that the biggies are just spectacular looking men. And so far, I say they have performed very well on film. Blut I think that the public would really like to see some real gay men on top, too. I mean, I am glad to see Tom Chase, for example, on top, as far as popularity. He is a very sweet man.

MICKEY: You've been in so many videos already, what is your ultimate fantasy that you'd like to do that you haven't yet done?

COLE: What I think I would love to do on video is to work with someone, maybe like Ace Harden—who I think is one of the sexiest men alive—and do a mutual, two-man scene they don't interrupt. They don't say, "Do this or that," and they don't position you, they just stand back and let us go have sex together and let us get off and drift off into each other.

MICKEY: Nice. Any particular position?

COLE: Sixty-nine, maybe going back and forth and screwing, wherever it goes. I want to have sex with another man that is completely mutual. With a full-fledged, well-hung, big, nasty man.

MICKEY: So, your type is big, hairy, nasty guys?

COLE: Big nasty guys.

MICKEY: Hairier than you?

COLE: Yes.

MICKEY: Older guys like you, guys in their mid-30s and up, are what many studios have discovered the public wants to see more of in porn. What do you think of that?

COLE: I think that it is very fortuitous for me to accidentally be brought into this business at this time. My timing couldn't be better since the leather trend is coming back. The market, after many years, is tired of the wonderful, beautiful, West Hollywood, gorgeous man. I think trends in video are like anything else the pendulum swings in a full swing and eventually it swings in the other direction. It is a natural process.

MICKEY: What made you think that you could have sex on camera?

COLE: Well, I didn't think I could do it. Greg Day, a photographer out of San Francisco, helped me a great deal. Then, I was recommended to Hot House Entertainment.

MICKEY: Then you met Steven Scarborough. He is a handsome older man himself.

COLE: Steve Scarborough is more than handsome. And it came to be that I would do a film with him for his Plain Wrapped videos. He really fast-forwarded me about what this business was like. And I am very grateful to him.

MICKEY: Like what? What did he tell you?

Photo courtesy: Men of Odyssey

In **Family Values**

COLE: The nicest thing that Steve did for me is, before we were hired and he knew I had never done this before, he showed me a picture. This picture was of a set. It was taken about 40 feet back and 20 feet up in the air. And that enabled you to see all the screens, the set, lights and the eight or nine guys running all the cables, with the two little bodies on the bed. He showed it to me and it hit me. "Oh, my god, that is what it is going to look like." So it gave me a moment of pause and I had the opportunity to think and say "either I can do this or I can't do this."

And I said, "I think I can do this." But it was brilliant of him because I am sure there are many people who realize "I can't do this" from the picture. That's saving time and money for everyone. He treated me very well and walked me through what I had to do and taught me about cheating, and taught me about opening up, and letting the cameras in, and pacing my speed, and the rules of what you can say and what you can't say, and what you can do, and what you can't do. He gave me the fast-forward course on this business. And I can never, ever, ever say enough about that experience.

MICKEY: So you started off with Steven. Did he say anything to you about your future, such as, "Are you sure you want to do this because if you are ever going to run for President, if you are ever going to be a lawyer, this could be a problem?"

COLE: The whole subject came up. I actually have a professional job. There is a risk at this. I was stepping over the line of being a private individual to being, to some degree, a public commodity.

MICKEY: Yeah. You are out there.

COLE: You are out there. I believed that I would do one or two movies and go away and have a wonderful memory. But what is happening—I'm in awe. I'm humbly in awe of this and kind of just holding my breath and walking the walk and living a day at a time and enjoying the ride with no great—(*He tears up*)

If this ended today and nothing else ever happened, I have had one of the greatest experiences.

MICKEY: Well, I didn't mean to get emotional with you. That's a sweet side of you many people don't get to see.

I want to talk about all the directors you have been working with, too. So lets go in order. We did Scarborough. And then your next one was **Down on Me**, for Chi Chi LaRue.

COLE: Yes.

MICKEY: How did that come about?

COLE: After I had **Acres of Ass** under my belt, I decided maybe I would like to do another one. And actually another model, Paul Jefferies said, "Oh girl, you need to call Chi Chi LaRue, here is her address." So I put together some of these shots by Greg Day, some lasers, and I mailed them.

MICKEY: He really meant a lot to your career, this Greg. …

COLE: Yes, he sure did. I put some of his lasers together and I mailed them off to Chi Chi. I mean it seemed like it was 24 hours later, she says, "Can you be here? Blah blah blah blah blah. You are perfect for a part I have this great role for you."

I was nervous because now I knew I was entering into a different realm—with Steven it's big time, but it was a specialty film and I knew that what I could do what he wanted me to do. I had no problem doing sex. This is now another thing, I have to do much more traditional mainstream sex on film. I had to act! I was very nervous. But, she was wonderful.

She flew me to Palm Springs, treated me like gold.

MICKEY: And then you went from there to Studio 2000 and legendary John Travis for **Grease Guns 2**?

COLE: I hired an agent then.

MICKEY: And who was that?

COLE: Peter Scott.

MICKEY: And are you still with him?

COLE: Yes. And the reason is, I live on the East Coast and I have a career and if you want to succeed in this business either you or somebody else has to be connected in the market here. Because either you do it yourself—which is very possible to do but it takes a lot of time, a lot of money in doing prints, a lot of mailing and a lot of getting in-the-know. Or, you hire someone.

MICKEY: A lot of schmoozing around. A lot of parties and stuff.

COLE: Right. I can't do that. I live 3,000 miles away. So for me the logical choice for me to continue in this business was hire an agent. And he took a chance, 'cause at the time, right when I hired him he says "I have a hunch that real men are coming back into video." And he got me a Studio 2000 shoot with the wonderful John Travis.

MICKEY: So, tell me about working with this Hall of Famer, who discovered some of the biggest names in the business.

COLE: He is a perfectionist. The best way to describe how he shoots is that John has a beautiful crossword puzzle put together in his mind and he needs to go through each piece of that crossword puzzle and film it. This is hard work.

We are talking about matching hands, matching feet, matching tongues, matching dicks, and it was very different from anything else I had ever done before.

MICKEY: So it was really acting. How did that feel?

COLE: The acting part, the non-sexual dialogue, is coming along. It is really coming along every video I do.

MICKEY: What happened with the great directors at Catalina that made you realize all this?

COLE: They film in each line independently. They don't do a series of five or six lines. They set you up.

MICKEY: And that was with Brad Austin and Josh Eliot?

COLE: Yes, it's for **Catalinaville.** I had lines. Josh Eliot is wonderful, he sets it up, he sets up the camera, he tells you where to look, you run once through the line and you say it and it's done.

MICKEY: Have you ever had acting training?

COLE: No.

MICKEY: And, you've never done theater or anything like that?

COLE: No.

MICKEY: This is all totally new to you?

COLE: Yes.

MICKEY: Do you think you could do mainstream acting?

COLE: I wouldn't venture to go there yet.

MICKEY: Because you know, on movie sets that is how they do it. They do it line for line.

COLE: That's easy for me.

MICKEY: There's a lot of waiting around, though.

COLE: And there's not on porn? Come on, let's get real. If it is under four hours something went wrong. It didn't happen. 'Cause they don't even get the lighting set up in four hours.

MICKEY: So then you went to Bruce Cam at Titan Media for **Fallen Angel**? You work with everybody, it is incredible.

COLE: Oh, god, those guys [at Titan Media] are wonderful. They are like a family: you just come into a family and they take you in and make you feel comfortable and welcomed. It's not like they treat you like a star, they just treat you like gold.

MICKEY: Who are you doing a scene with there?

COLE: I do a scene in a bathhouse with two guys. I did a couple of great scenes. It was so undirected: we were let free to have sex. And maybe they didn't get the perfect angle and the perfect this or that at any given moment but they got pure sexual energy. They got the real thing on tape, you know. In both scenes.

MICKEY: Tell me about working with Josh Eliot on the big Catalina project, **Catalinaville**? Is the studio as fabulous as everyone says it is?

COLE: Uh huh. Yes it is.

MICKEY: What are you doing in that?

COLE: I am the body guard to the main man who has the videotape that Steve Rambo steals and we could all go to jail. It's the first time on film that I show that I am versatile.

MICKEY: Is that how you are in real life?

COLE: I am a versatile actor and I am versatile in real life and I realize, the best way for me to represent my sexuality is to be true to myself and be honest on film. Giving pleasure to another man is why I get in bed, and what that takes is what it takes. I don't have this bottom/top thing.

MICKEY: See, you could have fallen into that very easily. This "I am only a top" kind of thing. You know how that is, you are big and rugged and there are very few guys like you who will bottom because there is a perception that it's a soft thing to do.

COLE: Well, when the stuff comes out and you see it on film, you are going to see something you haven't seen before. There are a few people like Donnie Russo, who take it like a man, and show what it is to please another man. You see, I think it's masculine to please another man and nothing it takes to please someone you care about and want to be in bed with and have sex with is feminine or degrading. You are a partner, you are a male partner engaging in manly sex. And that's how I see it.

MICKEY: Something that I noticed about you that is a very rare thing, I haven't seen it since probably York Powers, is that you are excellent at your own hot, nasty dialogue. Is this something that you've had to practice?

COLE: No. When I am in my private world and I am having sex, this is how I relate to the men who I am with and want to be related to that way. I will have sex how it is comfortable for me; the words, I don't think them up before, I don't know if you can tell that. They come spontaneously, it's what's going on, it's what turns me on. And I love to hear it back.

MICKEY: So, you like dirty talk?

COLE: Oh, yes.

MICKEY: Do people do it to you, too?

COLE: Oh, yes. Oh, please. And if you are a mute, do it with your hands. On the set with Steven Scarborough we were doing a scene and I am with a bearded guy and I am going, "Come on, come on baby, take it," and I hear "Cut!"

MICKEY: No babies.

COLE: Right. And from the other room I hear, "We're sorry, Cole, we forgot to tell you: you can't use the word baby."

I went, "Why?"

And he says, "Because with some of the distributors it implies pedophilia."

The man has a beard. It doesn't matter. I don't get it. So, there are many, many things that have to do with "boy" you can't use anymore.

MICKEY: What about "god"?

COLE: No. You can't use god, unfortunately. And I've said that. The music gets loud—guys, if you ever hear the music get loud, somebody said something that some distributor doesn't want. Read their lips.

MICKEY: Your first experience with fans was at the Probe Men in Video awards this year, right?

COLE: Yes, that was a great and difficult experience. These are not foundations to create who you are. It comes from inside you as a human being.

MICKEY: You seem refreshingly level-headed.

COLE: At 44 years old, who in their right mind, would ever fantasize that this could happen? When someone deals you a royal flush for the second time in your life and you don't bet on it, you are crazy.

The Bare Facts

Birthday: October 23, 1953
Zodiac Sign: Scorpio
Chinese Zodiac: Snake
Hair: Blond
Eyes: Brown
Height: 6-foot, 2-inches
Weight: 225 pounds
Cock Size: 9 1/2 inches
Favorite Color: Teal
Born: New York, NY.
Resides: Boston, Mass.
Workout Schedule: Two hours, six days a week.

Videography

Acres of Ass 1, *Plain Wrapped*
Acres of Ass 2, *Plain Wrapped*
Catalinaville, *Catalina Video*
Down on Me, *Mustang*
Fallen Angel, *Titan Media*
Family Values, *Men of Odyssey*
Grease Guns 2, *Studio 2000*
Leather Obsession 6:
   The Search, *Forum Studios*
Ramrod, *Catalina Video*
Slick, *Catalina Video*

Photo courtesy: Catalina Video

In **Catalinaville**

Video Renters' & Buyers' Guide

All Worlds Video
PO Box 33324
San Diego, CA 92163-9986
800-537-8024 or 619-298-8801
E-mail:
Development@Allworldsvideo.com

Bacchus Releasing
9980 Glenoaks Blvd. Unit C,
Sun Valley, CA 91352
(800) 923-7355 (818) 768-9101
E-mail: bacchusm@ix.netcom.com

Bel Ami
484-B Washington St. #342
Monterey, CA 93940-3030
(888) 442-9843
E-mail: gayvid@gayvid.com

BIG Entertainment
Post Office Box 550,
Hollywood, CA 90078-0550
(800) 359-0320 213-969-9800
E-mail: Bigv@bigvideo.com

Birlynn Productions
(212) 643-1636

Blade Productions see **Video 10**

Brick House Entertainment
7075 1/2 Vineland Avenue
North Hollywood, CA 91605
(818) 764-9890
FAX (818) 764-9821

E-mail: twistedv@aol.com; Website:
http://www.twistedvideo.com

Brush Creek Media
2215-R Market St., #148
San Francisco, CA, 94114
(415) 552-1506 FAX: (415) 552-3244
(800) 234-3877
E-mail: bcmsales@brushcreek.com

Campfire Videos
P.O Box 444487
Panorama City, CA 91412
(818) 891-5660 FAX: (818) 891-9605

Catalina Video
7985 Santa Monica Blvd. #109-G
W. Hollywood, CA 90046-5112
800-562-1897 or (818) 708-9200
FAX: (818) 708-3160
E-mail: catmendo@catalinavideo.com

Cazzo Films see **Video 10**

Centaur Films
2301 Sunset Plaza Dr.
(800) 446-8843 FAX: (818) 752-5065
(800) 446-8843
E-mail: Webmaster@centaurfilms.com;
Website: http://www.centaurfilms.com

Club 1821 see **Video 10**

Deluxe Entertainment see
Forum Studios

Dirty Dutchman see **Hot House**

Eruptions Video see **Hot House**

Euroman Video see **Hollywood Sales**

Falcon International see
Falcon Studios

Falcon Studios
Post Office Box 880906
San Francisco, California 94188-0906
(800) 227-3717
In California: (415) 431-7722
FAX: (415) 431-0127, E-mail:
customerservice@hawk.falconstudios.com
Website: http://www.falconstudios.com

Fat Dog Productions
8975 Fulbright Ave.
Chatsworth, CA 91311
(818) 727-7140 (800) 223-9461

Forum Studios
7985 Santa Monica #109-412
West Hollywood, CA 90046
(213) 871-6921
E-mail: info@forumstudios.com

French Films
Vidmax 1818 S. Industrial Road, #201,
Las Vegas, NV 89109

Galaxy Pictures see **Video 10**

HIS Video Gold
9650 De Soto Ave.
Chatsworth, CA. 91311-5012
(800) 458-4336 (818) 718-0202
FAX: (818) 718-8536
Website: http://www.hisweb.com

Hollywood Sales
P.O. Box 93969
Hollywood, CA. 91605
(800) 562-5428 FAX: (818) 255-0036
E-mail: videos@hollywoodsales.com
Website:
http://www.hollywoodsales.com/videos

Hot House Entertainment
P.O. Box 410990 #523
San Francisco, CA 914141-0990
(800) 884-4687 FAX: 415-864-8916
E-mail: hothouse@eyecon.com

International Media Distributors
(800) 733-3393

Island Caprice see **Video 10**

Jaguar Studios
3333 Glendale Blvd. #3
Los Angeles, CA 90039
(213) 663-8754

Jet Set Productions see
Brick House Entertainment

Jocks Studios see **Falcon Studios**

Kristen Bjorn Productions
P.O. Box 2520, SW 22nd St. #2-213
Miami, FL 33145
(800) 918-9130

Leather Entertainment see
Forum Studios
Leisure Time Entertainment
7050 Valjean Ave.
Van Nuys, CA. 91406
(818) 781-2345
FAX: (818) 781-3345

Marcostudio see **Video 10**

Mel Roberts International
1669 N. Beverly Glen Blvd.
Los Angeles, CA. 90077-2707

Men of Odyssey
P.O. Box 18589, Los Angeles, CA 90018
(800) 397-5114 (310) 202-0880
FAX: (310) 202-0897
Website: http://www.sex.se

Midnight Men see **Midnight Video**

Midnight Video
9158 Eton Ave.
Chatsworth, CA 91311
(818) 772-4201 (800) 298-3237
Website: www.midvid.com

Minotaur see **Studio 2000**

Mustang Studios see
Falcon Studios

New Age Pictures see
HIS Video Gold and **IMD**

Nubian Video see **Video 10**

O Men Video see
Men of Odyssey

Oh Man! Studios
8424 A Santa Monica Blvd., Suite 743
West Hollywood, CA 90069
(888) 442-9843
E-mail: webmaster@ohmanstudios.com

Plain Wrapped Video see
Hot House

Pleasure Productions
P.O. Box 946, 59 Laire Drive
Highstown, NJ
(908) 308-1777 (800) 999-2483

Pride Video
456 Sylvan Ave.
Englewood Cliffs, NJ 07632
(201) 569-1385

RedBoard Video
P.O. Box 2069
San Francisco, CA. 94126-2069
(415) 243-9606 FAX: (415) 243-9611
Website: http://www.redboard.com

Rough House see **Hot House**

Sarajava Productions see
Kristen Bjorn Productions

Sex Video see **Video 10**

Sierra Pacific Productions
PO Box 12109
Marina Del Rey, CA 90295
(800) 828-4336 FAX (310) 399-4770
E-mail: thor@thorsss.com
Website: http://www.thorsss.com

Studio 2000
7510 Sunset Blvd., Suite 1437
Hollywood, CA. 90046
(800) 435-2445
Website:
http://www.studio20004men.com

SX Films see **Video 10**

THOR Productions see
Sierra Pacific

Titan Media
P.O. Box 420099
San Francisco, CA 94142
(800) 360-7204
E-mail: titanteam@titanmedia.com

Totally Tasteless Video see
Totally Tight Video

Totally Tight Video
12420 Montague St, #D
Arleta, CA 91331
(818) 896-4321 (800) 923-7355
FAX (818) 768-9660

Video 10
7063 Lexington Ave.
West Hollywood, CA 90038
(213) 962-8504 (800) 548-4310
FAX: (213) 962-6489

Vivid Man
15127 Califa St.
Van Nuys, CA 91411
(818) 908-0481 (800) 423-4227
Website: http://www.vividman.com

Vivid Man Raw see **Vivid Man**

About the Author

FOR THE PAST DECADE, MICKEY SKEE (pictured below with Adam Rom, left, and Sonny Markham, right) has been known as one of the leading authorities on the ins-and-outs of the gay adult video industry.

He began as an erotic fiction writer, then, after reviewing porn tapes for *Thrust* and *Skin* magazines—in order to help out a friend—he was named Gay & Bi Editor of *Adult Video News*. Later, he started *Urge* magazine and is now editor-in-chief of *The Gay Film Magazine*.

His previous adult-industry books include, *The Films Of Ken Ryker*, published in 1997, and *The Best Of Gay Adult Video* 1998, both by Companion Press. Look for Mickey's work also in the *First Hand* anthologies, *Fresh Men, Manshots, Blueboy, Advocate Men, Jock, Obsessions, Infinity* and *All Men*.

Companion Press **ORDER FORM**

PAYMENT METHODS

U.S. Orders: Visa, MasterCard, American Exp. & MOs (Allow 2-4 weeks for delivery). Checks (Allow 6-8 weeks for delivery).
Canadian Orders: Visa/MC ONLY (Allow 4-6 weeks for delivery).
Overseas Orders: Visa/MC ONLY (Allow 4-6 weeks for delivery).

SHIPPING AND HANDLING

U.S. Orders: First item $3.00. $1.00 for each additional item.
Canadian Orders: First item $6.00. $1.00 for each additional item.
Overseas Orders: First item $20.00. $1.00 for each additional item.

HOW TO ORDER

Fax Orders: (949) 362-4489
E-Mail Orders: sstewart@companionpress.com
Website Orders: Order at www.companionpress.com
Mail Orders: Companion Press, PO Box 2575, Laguna Hills, California 92654
Phone Orders: (949) 362-9726 For questions and local calls

   Orders Only 1-800-373-0759
Mon.-Fri. 8 AM - 3 PM Pacific Standard Time

Qty	ISBN # last 3 digits only	Title	Price (each)	Price

PRINT Name _____
You must also sign age consent statement below
Address _____

City _____ State____ Zip _____

Phone ( ) _____
For questions about your order

Discount or Credit	
CA Residents add 7.75% Sales Tax	
Shipping & Handling **See above for rates**	
TOTAL	

Payment Method ❑ Check (U.S. currency only—allow 6-8 wks.), make payable to COMPANION PRESS.
❑ Visa ❑ MasterCard ❑ American Express ❑ Money Order

Credit card # _____ Exp. date _____

X **Signature** Required for all orders

I certify by my signature that I am over 21 years old and desire to receive sexually-oriented material. My signature here also authorizes my credit card charge if I am paying for my order by Visa, MasterCard or American Express.

698